EDUCATING THE INTELLIGENT CHILD

EDUCATING THE INTELLIGENT CHILD

Victor Serebriakoff

MENSA

Published by Mensa Publications,
9 Hinton Road, Fulbourn,
Cambridge CB1 5DZ

Copyright © Victor Serebriakoff 1990

British Library Cataloguing in Publication Data
Serebriakoff, Victor, 1912–
    Educating the intelligent child.
    1. Exceptional children. Education
    I. Title
    371.9

ISBN 1-872122-20-5

Cover design by Dale Dawson

Designed by Dale Dawson in association with
Book Production Consultants, Cambridge

Typeset by KeyStar, St. Ives, Cambridge

Printed and Bound in the U.K. by Redwood Press, Melksham

NOTE: All opinions expressed in this book are those of the
author and are not endorsed by British Mensa Ltd which has
no corporate view.

Contents

Chapter 1

The variability of education

THOSE INTERESTED IN promising children are bound to be interested in education. The best in British education today is as good as, maybe better than, anything anywhere. The worst is very bad indeed.

The British Government commands that every child shall spend about ten years, ten thousand precious childhood hours, in full time education. What are the results? What does this enormous, expanding, expensive, national effort by nearly a million professional educationalists and 12 million children produce?

At one extreme, some of the most distinguished, brilliant, effective and highly-educated people in the world. Britain, for its size, can hold its head high as regards the contribution to the world culture of the brilliant and influential scholars, inventors, scientists, writers and savants of every type who have been educated here. We have proportionately more Nobel Prize winners than any other nation.

But, at the other end of the scale, the school system delivers into the labour market every year terrifyingly large numbers of innumerate, illiterate youngsters who find it very difficult to fit into a contributory role in the comfortable, affluent, technology based, industrial lifestyle which the work over centuries of those at the other end of this scale has made possible.

The levels of literacy in some Midland schools have been found to be equivalent to those of the inmates of the workhouses in 1840 according to Rodney Atkinson in his latest book.

Unemployment recently has been as high as three million and it is still over half that figure (1989). And significantly, a high proportion of those who spend miserable years in a non-contributing role are the badly-educated and undertrained. Here is an enormous national educational failure.

The professionals, the various interest groups who provide this patchy, imperfect service to the nation all have their own explanations. On the media they are vociferous but they rarely question their own ideas, methods and efforts. Those who accept that things are not as good as they can be, blame every group but themselves. Most blame the government and vociferously join the long queue of supplicants leading to the taxpayer's pocket. All would be well, they persuasively argue, if only we dug deeper and provided more 'funding' or 'resources' (nothing so vulgar as money).

The great variability of state funded education under local authority control in Britain is amply demonstrated by a report called *The School Effect* published by the Policy Studies Institute in 1989. Since 1981, 3000 pupils aged 11 to 16 in 20 urban comprehensive schools were investigated in a long-term study. Between 10 and 80 per cent of the pupils in urban schools chosen were from ethnic minority groups. The researchers, David J. Smith and Sally Tomlinson, reported very great variability in educational results even when all allowance was made for the initial social and ethnic differences between the children. One of their conclusions was that, as regards mathematics and reading progress, the school a child goes to is more important than the ethnic or social group to which he or she belongs. The differences were extreme, so great that a given child would be likely to get a B grade O level at one school but no better than a third level CSE at another. At the first school the child might be a candidate for good A levels and a university place, in the wrong school they would be a drop out, an educational reject.

They point to enormous differences in the styles of organisation of schools and these seem to result in the enormous variability of outcome much more than the variability of the pupils themselves.

The failure of the British educational system to develop British talent is further illustrated by a recent report by Mr John Butcher (junior education minister at the time) in which he admitted that British students were up to two years behind their German counterparts in mathematics. Similarly poor comparative results show a serious deficit in the average performance of British students against scholars in certain other countries such as Japan and France. The evidence applies to the gross average performance. The evidence above points to very great *variability* of results in Britain. Our best results are as good as anything anywhere. If the best results are good and the average very poor it seems to follow that the results at the lower end of the scale are abysmal. The complacency we so often hear from some teachers and teachers' unions about the educational methods of today seems to be unjustified.

A report from the school inspectorate this year (1989) also admits that one in four primary state schools is failing to teach mathematics in a satisfactory manner. They also note that too much time is given to practising skills which have already been mastered and too little to progress, and they make many other criticisms.

It is difficult not to worry about the declining standards in some areas of British education when we read the string of press reports about the absurd ignorance of some students who have graduated from our universities.

We have to wonder how far up the system weakness of the 'no labelling, no failures' philosophy has spread. One report in the *Sunday Times* (25.6.89) states that large employers' faith in graduate examinations was so much undermined that they were setting up their own 'graduate appraisal service'. Eleven companies including Shell, British Aerospace and Abbey National are involved. The appraisal's first findings indicate that more than 40 per cent of graduates were not sufficiently numerate to 'reduce 10,000 by 80 per cent'. Twelve and a half per cent could not work out a simple average. Very poor spelling among those who had obtained honours degrees was also frequently seen.

The universities should be on their guard to protect the value of the qualifications they award. If they fail to maintain the public and particularly the employers' faith in the value of their examinations then market forces will cause two things to happen. Firstly, other competitive systems of certification or quality control will arise. They will be more useful and informative to those who have to choose people for jobs. Secondly, the urge to attend universities that give out unvalued qualifications will decline. Young people go to universities to get degrees, they get a lot more we hope, but we must never forget the primary incentive. The less the perceived value of the degree, the less they will desire it.

Another frightening indication of the damage done by the un-researched changes in educational practice that have been introduced is the great decline in knowledge of geography which is manifest. A *Sunday Times* investigation reported in April 1989 revealed that a quarter of 11-year-olds could not find Russia on a globe. The same proportion failed to find France, our nearest southern neighbour. Half could not find the biggest feature on the globe, the Pacific Ocean. In a country where many people travel abroad each year the neglect of geography teaching is surely a great mistake.

Now much of the education industry has accepted the egalitarian paradigm and the bulk of today's heads and teachers have been taught to believe or pay lip service to the principle that all children have equal potential and therefore should be treated alike. We are therefore entitled to ask them and ourselves for an explanation of these staggering differences between the worst educational results and the best. We have to try to make sense of it all.

Things in education are bad but I can be of some small comfort to teachers and the rest of us. The teachers need not accept *all* the blame for the enormous variability of their output. There are certainly causes within their control but there are some beyond it. There is no need to accept the implausible case, so glibly and indignantly put, that all differences are due to 'social inequalities' or 'deprivation'. They must have observed that the inequalities of educability are to be seen in all social strata. Upper class, middle class, working class, deprived class, 'underprivileged minorities'; all have the full range of educational achievement. All have scholars and slow learners.

Children are different

The ideas in this chapter would have seemed obvious to most past generations but it is sadly necessary to start by reaffirming them because that other set of ideas has become quite popular and influential since the intellectual anarchy of the silly '60s.

Bright children start as babies and anyone who has had dealings with babies for any time will know that though they are all small, look alike and have about the usual number of limbs and things, they are all, right from birth, individuals which differ from one another in many ways. The exceptions, one birth in about 500, prove the rule. Uniovular (one egg) twins, seem most unusual just because of their extraordinary similarity.

Further experience of growing children shows us that the differences babies are born with tend to develop rather than diminish as they grow older. So when the babies finally get to be adults we experience the rich, rewarding and beautiful diversity of humanity.

Babies and the people they grow to be differ in height, weight, colour, health, behaviour, appearance, intelligence, and a thousand other ways.

Why? There are many millions of species of animals on Earth and it is probable that they all came from one original form, the primaeval protozoan. Evolutionary theory explains two things. One is the similarity of the animals within a species, the other is the great differences between the species. The evolutionary theory tells us that despite the similarities of the animals within a species that every one of them is different from all the others in that species in many ways, so that fundamentally, each is unique. In fact the big differences between species arise from these small ones within species. The difference between the oak tree and the otter, the elephant and the eel, arose from these small differences forking out over a very long time. So men and women, like all other creatures, have many resemblances but many differences too.

Differences in educability

Among the many differences between people there are undoubted differences in their educability, the amount of education they can absorb and the speed at which they can absorb it. The subject of this book is those at the top end of this scale. A source book in this field is one which has never been circulated to the general public. What has been called 'The Marland Report' was commissioned by Senator S. P. Marland Jnr, at that time the Commissioner for Education in the USA. It is the Report to the Congress, *Education Of The Gifted and Talented* and I shall quote from it in this book. Recommendations were invited from 230 experts in this field. The book is the summary of their views.

It would be right to quote the first sentence in this important report which was inspired by the worry in the USA when the Russians gained the first initiative in the space race.

"Executive summary

BACKGROUND AND METHODOLOGY OF THE STUDY

Educators, legislators, and parents have long puzzled over the problem of educating gifted students in a public educational program geared primarily to a philosophy of egalitarianism.

We know that gifted children can be identified as early as the pre-school grades and that these children in later life often make outstanding contributions to our society in the arts, politics, business and the sciences. But, disturbingly, research has confirmed that many talented children perform far below their intellectual potential. We are increasingly being stripped of the comfortable notion that a bright mind will make its own way. Intellectual and creative talent cannot survive educational neglect and apathy.

This loss is particularly evident in the minority groups who have in both social and educational environments every configuration calculated to stifle potential talent."

There follow three more quotations.

"Gifted and talented youth are a unique population, differing markedly from their age peers in abilities, talents, interests, and psychological maturity. They are the most versatile and complex of all human groups, possibly the most neglected of all groups with special educational needs. Their sensitivity to others and insight into existing school conditions make them especially vulnerable, because of their ability to conceal their giftedness in standardized surroundings and to seek alternative outlets. The resultant waste is tragic.

"Research studies on special needs of the gifted and talented demonstrate the need for special programs. Contrary to widespread belief, these students cannot ordinarily excel without assistance. The relatively few gifted students who have had the advantage of special programs have shown remarkable improvements in self-understanding and in ability to relate well to others, as well as in improved academic and creative performance. The programs have not produced arrogant, selfish snobs; special programs have extended a sense of reality, wholesome humility, self-respect, and respect for others. A good program for the gifted increases their involvement and interest in learning through the reduction of the irrelevant and redundant. These statements do not imply in any way a 'track system' for the gifted and talented.

"The assumption that the gifted and talented come from privileged environments is erroneous. Even in the Terman study, which made no pretense of comprehensive search and identification, some participants came from economically deprived homes while the majority came from homes with certain advantages; the Terman group included representatives of all ethnic groups and all economic levels, with 19 per cent of the parents representing skilled and unskilled labor.

"A later California study (a more thorough but by no means complete

11

search for gifted children in certain rural sections) found that 30 per cent of parents were in agricultural, clerical, service, semi-skilled, unskilled, semi-professional, or sales occupations. Jenkins found an incidence of nearly one per cent of gifted Negroes in segregated Chicago school classes in the early 1940's, despite his extremely limited screening and referral procedures.

"Even though the major studies have not employed detailed community searches, giftedness has been found in all walks of life.

"Obviously, we can identify giftedness – or it identifies itself, particularly when a 2-year-old begins to read or play the piano. But identification is really much more complicated. It includes many factors: 1) age of identification (given the well-known sensitivity and adjustability of the gifted, how is it identified after the child has learned to conceal it to survive happily among his peers?); 2) screening procedures and test accuracy; 3) the identification of children from a variety of ethnic groups and cultures; and 4) tests of creativity (before that creativity has been demonstrated in performance). What then is our capacity to locate the gifted and talented within the school population?

"On the basis of both early and current studies, we can identify these children, quite apart from their tendency to emerge at times on their own. Attempts to identify gifted children through tests at the kindergarten level have been successful when careful preliminary search and screening have been utilized.

"Although much has been said about the low relationship between infant tests and those used during the school years, infant tests are primarily motor tests; later tests emphasize verbal abilities."

Can we identify the gifted person from minorities and divergent cultures?

"In 1940 Paul Witty summarized published studies dealing with the relationship of Negro and white ancestry to intelligence. He concluded that the studies from 1916 to the time of his report were inconclusive and that while there were differences in subgroups within each race, there were no true racial differences in intelligence (184).

"A 1940 doctoral study by Jenkins systematically searched for gifted Negro children in grades three through eight, in seven Chicago public schools which enrolled approximately 8,000 Negro children. The search employed teacher nomination, group testing, and ultimately Stanford-Binet examination of every child with a group test I.Q. of 120 or more. Jenkins found that one school failed to identify a single gifted child, and that the percentages of gifted children (I.Q. 140 or above) ranged from .83 to .41 in the seven schools (85). One girl had an I.Q. of 200. Contrary to Terman's findings, Jenkins found a proportion of 2.33 girls to one boy. In a study he found traits similar to those described in other groups of children with superior intelligence: well educated parents, superior advancement developmentally, and desirable personality traits (87).

Eighty per cent of the experts mentioned included those with high general intellectual ability in the 'gifted and talented' categories. The same proportion favoured multiple screening and search (60 per cent said at least annually), to identify them during education.

"The advocates favoured the use of multiple means for identification of the gifted and talented, including measures of intelligence, achievement, talent, and creativity. The highest rank was accorded the individual intelligence test, a means presently not used in most States because of the cost involved. (Group measures fail to locate half of the gifted and talented in any population.)

"Apparently the advocates were concerned by the failure of school personnel to identify the gifted, as well as by the well-known ability of the gifted to conceal their true abilities and to adapt themselves to school offerings and requirements. Reports, such as those of the 57.5 per cent of schools nationally stating in the *School Staffing Survey* that they had *no* gifted pupils, undoubtedly led the respondents to recommend involvement of all persons in the search process. School psychologists were seen as most important, with talent specialists next."

Now these quotations apply to an American investigation but the whole report seems to be addressing what has been an transatlantic problem. There is no comparative report for Britain but it would be rash to say that none of the problems in America arise in Britain.

We have to work together

If we accept that there are going to be great and unavoidable differences in educational outcome we must still remember that Homo sapiens, our species, is a social animal. We live, work and play together in social groups, families, firms, institutions, nations, all in social co-operation with each other. However, we are, each of us, autonomous. We have free will. And like all other animals, even social animals, we are competitive. So we all have to be pretty skilful at understanding the character and peculiarities of those around us. Thus we know what to expect from each other and how to get things done together in the strange but very effective, competitive co-operative systems which we have gradually built up between us. We manage this constant adjustment to each other, this finely balanced competing co-operation very well. So well that we sometimes take these complex social insights and skills for granted. Despite the extent of human diversity we manage to get on together and sort out who is best at what. Thus we knit together the complex, social, communication fabrics upon which all human beings depend for their existence. We are so used to worrying about and deploring the exceptions, the times when this neatly dovetailed, contending co-operation breaks down, that we forget the miraculous way in which it all works nearly all the time.

A very important human difference

I have emphasised the many ways that humans differ from babyhood onwards but in this book I am most concerned with just one of them. I am concerned about this sort of difference because it is very important and growing more so as this particular civilisation advances. I am also concerned because in some circles, just at the moment when it is so important, there is a fashionable error which suggests that this particular difference is unimportant or does not exist. Those who are seized of this error seem to have made a slip of the mind. I think it is a socially damaging one.

It is to this difference we have to look if we are to explain the great differences in educability mentioned above.

You will have guessed the differences I refer to, they are the differences in intelligence between babies, children, people. In Europe we live in a culture which is based on the excellent principles of equality before the law, equality of opportunity and equal entitlement to state welfare benefits for those that need them. But some people seem to feel that from these excellent qualities it follows that people are in fact all like one-egg twins or clone mates, all alike in character and potential and that it makes sense for us all to treat each other as such.

Now these people have had the same experience of dealing with human differences as we all have, and are undoubtedly as good as we are at the delicate competitive cooperative juggling described above. So they are good at the old human trick of believing in two opposite ideas at the same time. Now that is quite OK in many cases because it is quite usual to have one idea which determines what we say and another which determines our actions. We all combine petty dishonesties with a declared respect for honesty and so on. As long as those who believe in the clone-like equality of mankind continue to pay only lip-service to this belief and behave to people according to their adjudged different characteristics all will be well. But there is one sphere in which these peculiar inhuman ideas about humanity actually do guide behaviour. It is in the sphere of education, a very important one, and that is what worries me and set me writing this book.

Some unpopular facts

We have to look at three not very acceptable facts. Some children are born with a quick and active enquiring turn of mind and can soon be seen to be forward, precocious, bright, gifted, clever, there are many ways of describing the way they behave. They seem to learn quickly and well, are beginning to use a few words by the time they are eight months old and compose short sentences by the time they are 18 months. They can often read quite well long before they go to school, as early as three years, sometimes even much earlier. At the other end of the scale there are children we prefer not to think about. There are a tiny minority of very retarded children who never even learn to feed themselves or walk. These cases sometimes arise from accidents before or during birth but not always. Then there are those who are very slow to talk, some never learning at all. As we go up this unhappy scale we find those where it is very difficult to teach them to read even when they become adults. Many remain illiterate. These children are precious humans, usually loving and lovable but they are handicapped and need our support and help. The next fact we have to face is the most difficult.

THE NORMAL CURVE

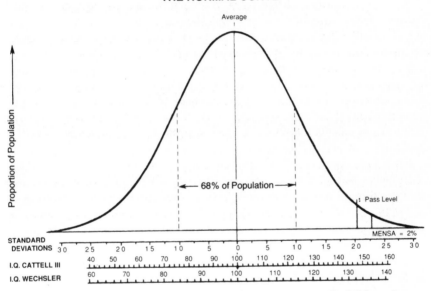

It is an error to lump all these 'mentally handicapped' children into a single category because there is no sharp dividing line in this progression of teachability and intelligence. It is a smooth gradient from the extremely retarded child up through all levels of ability to the very able, fast learning and precocious child who may become a genius if it has the incentives and the opportunities. Fortunately there are very few severely retarded children. The nearer you get to the average the more of each sort there are. Unfortunately there are equally few of the very advanced ones also. These are the ones that modern societies need much more than primitive ones did.

Every population can be arranged on the normal curve, the bell curve discovered by Gauss, which regulates the distribution of many aspects of living systems.

This is the bell curve showing the distribution of a variable like intelligence quotient in the population. Most cluster near the average in score, ie 100. The further we get from the average the less examples you get with that score.

It would be nice to believe, as many manage to do, that people are comfortably average and normal except for a few 'accidents' at the lower extreme. The rest are 'normal' and can do anything if only they try hard enough and are treated right. It would be nice to believe it but quite wrong and harmful to do so. The world is not like that at all. We have to adjust to the unpopular truth that though a few enlightened societies confer equal *rights* to their citizens, they are born unequal and there is no way to make them equal in comprehension, achievement and contribution. Like it or not, some are going to be able to do very difficult and demanding jobs very well for the general benefit. Others are not going to be able to find a way to make any contribution at all. And in modern societies the inequality of contribution is becoming greater. In advanced societies we depend much more than we did on a minority of highly talented, strongly motivated, well educated, trained and hard-working experts. We depend less than we did on the serried ranks of manual workers doing repetitive work in manufacture and agriculture, more upon designers and inventors, setters and maintainers of the automatic machines which are replacing the former. If we see these things clearly we shall manage things better and have fewer miserable and frustrated people around. We can better ensure a good life for all if we recognise, take account of and socially utilise our differences than if we pretend them away.

Modern civilised life can make a living space for all kinds of talents and abilities but the job of getting various shaped pegs into suitable holes is getting more difficult. It will not be made easier if the present fashion of trying to pretend that all the pegs are exactly the same shape, or can be made to be so, continues.

We need to return to the traditional practice of recognising and working with the grain of human diversity rather than trying to abolish it or pretend it ain't so. Luckily the tide of fashion is turning and we are moving away from the International Standard Clone-Person concept.

So we have to make judgments

In what follows I have to assume that the reader can accept that there is a need, in a highly variable social animal, to know or make good guesses about the characteristics, the strengths and the weaknesses of the members of a society if only for the purpose of fitting the members into it in the most beneficial way. I must emphasise that the 'need to know' envisaged is the right of individuals and institutions to make judgments about and know about those they depend on and work with. I do not like the idea of centralised records of such information except in the cases where it is obviously socially essential. Criminal records and health records are examples of justified central records of the characteristics of people. Even they must be used with confidential care and justice.

Once we accept that groups need to judge some of their neighbours and colleagues, the better to fit in with them co-operatively, we shall obviously want to find the fairest methods of doing so.

New social styles

The family and the hunter-gatherer tribe were the only social units known to mankind for some millions of years up until 6–8,000 years ago. It is for these traditional kinds of organisation that human instincts and character-istics were 'designed', as it were.

The family group and the tribal group, that is the most 'natural' group for humanity, is a mixed age, mixed sex group. (There is a tendency in some primitive tribes to segregate sexes and ages at certain periods in con-nection with rites of passage but the general pattern is to mix all ages together in tribal and family life.)

The hunter-gatherer tribal pattern described above is obsolete except in a few dwindling areas off the beaten track. But all our more complex in-stitutions have to work with an emotional and instinctual background, in mankind, which was right for these earlier lifestyles. In much of the world we now have an enormous interwoven structure of social institutions and we have to learn to work it with the same instinctual equipment, the same pleasure-pain system that guided us for millions of years. This creates many problems of course.

The family and the tribe knew each other face to face. They had devel-oped an excellent system for making and communicating judgments about their tribe fellows. All languages have a rich pattern of words which describe character and personality. These useful words express expecta-tions of how individuals will perform in various circumstances. Tribes judged people on scales of brave/cowardly, hard-working/idle, skilful/ clumsy, generous/stingy, kind/cruel, strong/weak, clever/stupid, aggres-sive/submissive. The list is as long as your arm. And these classifications and judgments were vital to the success and viability of the tribe in competition with those around it.

Now the lifestyle of most of humanity has changed utterly and it is likely that there has been a change in the relative importance of these scales (or parameters) of human difference. Virtues and vices which are vital to wandering hunters become less important to people who live in complex industrial societies. And vice versa. So we should expect a great change in the ways of judging people today.

Applying science to judgment

Further, the industrial lifestyle arises from the discovery and the develop-ment of the scientific method. We should expect that science should be applied to the vital business of assessing people and their potentialities.

One difference between the scientific and other methods is that scientists try to deduce the general from the particular. They try to discover more general facts, those which are more widely applicable. Thus they use statistics, the art which seeks to produce useful generalisations from representative samples. A manufacturer of clothing finds it useful to know the average height and waist measurement of the population he serves. He also likes to know the range of variation from that average. The tribesman had to base his scales of judgment on each person around him. The statistician tries to base his scale on large populations.

There are some who oppose, verbally at least, the new industrial lifestyle I describe and assert that the more primitive style is more viable and preferable. But the feet vote a different way from the voices. Whatever they say, people tell us by their behaviour that they prefer the modern lifestyle. And we have to concede that it calls for a lot more people of very high cognitive intelligence. A tribe needs one wise old man and a brave and clever chief. A modern industrial society is designed to amplify the intelligence of a handful of experts so that it applies and serves human communities more widely. Inventors, entrepreneurs and experts of all kinds can cause whole industries to arise so that a good idea does not just benefit one firm, group or tribe but the whole of the developed world.

The human difference that is most important

I emphasise that the one human difference upon which I am going to concentrate in this book, human cognitive intelligence, has now become the most important one of all.

So without further apologies I shall now explain how this human speciality can be assessed and measured with a reasonable degree of confidence on a general statistical scale so that fair comparisons can be made over wide populations.

Before we go into measurement we have to clarify what it is we think we are measuring. Intelligence, nous, wit, wisdom, capacity, brightness, cleverness, genius, talent, sagacity, perspicacity, cunning, shrewdness, these are just some of the words that have got into our language to express the idea to be found in all societies and cultures, the universal idea of general intelligence. I have to say this because there are some political extremists who are committed to the idea that these words describe a non-entity, an unreal factor which has been invented by capitalistic academic exploiters so as to oppress the poor. Technically what we mean by measured general intelligence is the overall general ability to do well at a whole range of cognitive tasks, tasks which call for the acquisition, filtering, processing and manipulation of symbolic information and making optimum decisions based on it. (By symbolic information we mean that which can be passed between people in words, signs, diagrams, mathematical symbols and the like). The language assumes that intelligence is a unitary factor and Spearman's researches and many others have shown that it is.

Can we measure such a complex thing as intelligence?

The answer to this question that arises from research is, with reservations 'yes, with enough accuracy to be useful'.

There is a very important simplifying factor, the above discovery Spearman made, that cognitive ability is, as it were, 'unfairly' distributed. Cognitive abilities cluster, children that are good at one cognitive task tend, (over large samples, in general), to be good at all the others. Poor scorers at one task tend to be below average all round. Broadly it is true that some general human variable like cleverness or intelligence guides and informs how we perform across a very wide range of certain communicative skills and tasks. There is, contrary to our sense of justice and fairness, no law of compensation which ensures that if you are bad at one thing you are likely to be good at another. Quick learners and good thinkers tend to be quick and good at many tasks, slow learners are usually slow all round. In matters of ability, apparently 'To them that hath shall be given' applies. This seems to be Nature's way. It is perhaps not surprising that many people find this hard truth emotionally difficult to accept.

Of course, many other fine human qualities, bravery, kindness, unselfishness, loyalty, good nature, athletic prowess, grace, and moral worth are independent variables which do not correlate with intelligence. Broadly speaking, cognitive ability itself is just another one of these relatively independent unitary factors.

Statistically standardised tests

The art of mental testing is technically called psychometrics (*not* psychometry which has another meaning, one which is not academically respected).

It was probably Francis Galton who first conceived the idea of a statistical measure of human intelligence but the first intelligence test scales were produced by Alfred Binet in Paris who hit on the concept 'mental age'.

Think of a set of cognitive tasks, graded in ascending order of difficulty. (Recognition, reasoning, interpreting, comprehension, calculation, communication, these are examples of cognitive tasks. Dancing and playing tennis employ much less cognitive ability. They would not be used for IQ tests.)

Now test a large random sample of children all born the same day and eight years old now. Let them carry out the list of tasks as they get more difficult. Each child goes on until he cannot achieve any more. They will all fail at different points along the scale but the mid point in the range of scores, that where as many do better as there are that do worse will give you the medium performance for an eight year old child. Any child, (or person) regardless of age, who reaches but cannot pass that point is said to have a 'mental age' of eight. Now derive levels for six-year-olds, seven-year-olds, etc, in the same way. With that concept Binet could go on to rate the mental age against the actual age (or chronological age as he called it) so as to get a measure of mental advancement or retardation. If you now divide the mental age by the actual age you get a sort of measure of this. A ten-year-old child who has a mental age of 12 at the age of ten is said to have an 'intelligence ratio' of 1.2. (Terman later developed the IQ or 'Intelligence Quotient' by simply multiplying the result by 100 so as to get rid of the decimals). So our eight-year-old above had an IQ of 120. Thus we get the concepts of 'advancement' and 'retardation' in the field of psychometrics and psychiatry. It has proved to be clinically and educationally useful. In the educational field and only in that is it contentious.

From the above it will be seen that the 'average' IQ should be 100 and any figure below that represents some degree of retardation while any figure above 100 indicates advancement. These figures apply to some particular population and obviously that can only be gauged from samples of that population. And there is the rub. If one population of children speaks a different language or has been brought up in a very different way from another then the mental ages for the two groups are likely to be different on any test. The intelligence tests for one population become less valid for the other population. They do not become, as so many critics claim 'meaningless', but they become less reliable. A great deal has been made of this point, especially by those who detest the range of human diversity so much that it leads them into an 'I don't want to know' attitude towards any idea of mental measurement or any other judgments about people.

However, it is unwise to throw away your needles until you get a sewing machine. So while the only alternative to intelligence testing we know of is human judgment, with all its bias and uncertainty, we must try to overcome any cultural bias in intelligence tests, not condemn them out of hand. Human judgment is notoriously biased in many ways and must be based on even smaller and less representative samples. The alternative of educating children without making any judgments at all about their ability or handicap is obviously not open to us. We want our rulers, judges, engineers, doctors and other elites of experts to be rigorously selected for suitability and that means someone has to make good judgments about their capacity for education and training at various stages of their career. To select students suitable for advanced training and teaching courses we need some sort of filter which selects teachability (intelligence). We must use the best and fairest methods we know and, despite all the assertions to the contrary, intelligence tests are just that. Perfect they are not. Better, fairer ways we do not know. Teachers' assessment, experts' judgment, academic examinations, they all do a job. But research persistently shows that they do a worse job and are less fair. It is the children of immigrant minority culture groups that stand to gain most from a properly standardised, objective, testing system.

It is only the intelligence test that has even a chance of seeing through cultural differences to the underlying ability hidden beneath it. But we must bear in mind their limitations and make allowances when we use tests on groups they were not designed for.

Is intelligence a single factor?

The information we get from an intelligence test is the intelligence quotient; a single, simple scale. Good tests are based on very careful research on large random samples of the population concerned, they are carefully checked and validated against other measures. The whole process takes a long time and costs a great deal. That is why you cannot expect to see such tests available to the general public. They are obtainable only by trained professionals.

A single figure between about 50 for the severely retarded and about 200 for the exceptionally bright, expresses the general cognitive intelligence, versatility or teachability of the child or adult. From the IQ figure and a knowledge of the statistical characteristics of the test used we can derive other figures which are much more useful, the decile or percentile. They are much more easily understood. The decile divides the population into ten equal classes and tells you to which class the subject belongs. If a child was in the 5th decile it would be just below average. If in the first decile it is in the lowest tenth as regards IQ score and if it were on the ninth decile it would be in the top tenth. Percentiles work the same way except that the division is into 100 classes, each comprising one per cent of the population. To join Mensa you have to score on the 98th percentile so that you are in the top two per cent for IQ score.

How can you tell if your child is bright?

The answer to this question depends a lot on the age of the child. Broadly we can say two things:

1 The younger the child the *less* reliable and predictive is any attempt to measure its intelligence on a written or verbal test.

2 The brighter the child is the *more* reliable the test is. The usual practice adopted by educational psychologists is this. With average children, six is the youngest age at which to use an intelligence test on a child. But a very bright child of three and a half might have a six year mental age and could usefully be tested. It is not possible to publish a fully standardised test of intelligence in a book such as this because the publication of

the answers would devalue the test. But a first approximation test closely based on such a professional test is given at the end of the next chapter. I have to emphasise that an individual test by an expert is far the best method and even a group test by a trained person is preferable. But this test will give a 'better-than-nothing' first approximation estimate. You can arrange for a professional group test or an individual test for your child (and/or yourself, come to that) via Mensa. Just write to 'Mensa Freepost Wolverhampton' giving the child's age.˙

As to children below six years old, there are ways to test younger children but they require special skills and training. A professional paediatrician or educational psychologist can make good predictive guesstimates which are a lot better than nothing.

However, in very young babies there are things which any parent can watch out for which can give an early promise or warning of advancement or retardation. A table giving a guide as to what behavioural and perceptive skills can be expected at what ages will be given in Chapter 2. These can only be taken as a first rough approximation. Children will almost certainly lag on some tasks and be advanced on others. If the child cannot be motivated to take an interest the result will mean little.

The latest about testing young children

Every science is advancing and I now have to report a late amendment to what I have said above which indicates that a new method of testing very young children promises to give quite reliable predictions about intelligence measure from babyhood. As far as I know, at the time of writing the new method has not been practised in the UK but it seems to be accepted in the USA.

The claim is that tests performed on babies as young as six months old are proving to be very predictive of test scores achieved two years later. Dr Joseph Fagan of the Chase Western Reserve University found that early measures of motor skill were not predictive of later general intelligence, so he tried an ingenious test of visual memory based on the observed fact that young babies are interested and stimulated by novelty. They lost interest in familiar patterns and this is easily seen. Thus it is possible to find out how much exposure to a pattern or design is required to elicit the boredom reaction which show that it has been learned. The hypothesis was that quick learning is a measure of intelligence.

Dr Fagan claims that he predicted from these tests that 28 out of 55 babies in his first sample would be above average in later tests of IQ. He followed the babies for three years and found that he correctly identified 21 out of the 28 judging by the scores they got on the Revised Peabody Picture Vocabulary test.

Professor Feuerstein in Israel also claims to be able to test young children using tests of actual learning ability on a similar principle.

A much more promising development in this field arises from work started in the '60s by the Canadian psychologist, Professor Oertle, and now being developed by Professor Hans Eysenck. The subject's reaction time as shown on an electroencephalogram scan can be fed into a computer in such a way as to produce an objective measure of general intelligence even in very young babies. The results correlate highly with the other methods. There can be no question of cultural bias with such tests as they rely entirely on automatically sensed, involuntary reactions to a standard stimulus. It is possible that when these methods are perfected they will replace the uncertainties of present methods of IQ testing. Until they do the IQ test remains the best we have.

The case that intelligence is a 'reification' invented by the 'class enemy' especially to handicap the poor has been soberly advanced by some otherwise sensible academics. The above experiments already diminish the microscopic plausibility of this 'reification' view of the most human of human traits.

A complication

At this point I have to mention a complication. It should be clear that mental testing is not an exact art. Measuring thinking power is not like measuring height. It is much less exact. All scores should be looked at with caution and checked if there seems to be reason for doubt. Every tale we tell about the art is to some extent a simplification, and what is said above is that too. I have said that the assumptions of the language and of the work of Spearman have shown that intelligence is a unitary factor. This is nearly true but later research has shown that it is truer to say that it is two or perhaps more very closely related factors.

One factor seems to be connected with that ability to learn, use and comprehend language, verbal ability in fact. This has a very high association with general intelligence. The other factor is more complex. It relates to the subject's ability to comprehend three-dimensional space relations.

Those with one of these abilities are very likely to have the other but there is also a tendency for them to diverge. There are some very bright people who are slightly deficient on one of these two factors and make up for it on the other. This has an unhappy consequence. Space relations tests, those consisting mostly of diagrams, are thought to be much fairer to those who do not speak the test language so well.

Diagrammatic tests can be answered by most First and Second World language groups without great bias, since they deal with material which is fairly new to all the subjects. Diagram format is common to many cultures and language groups. But a purely diagrammatic test is slightly unfair to the subject who makes up for a deficit in space relations comprehension with a higher degree of verbal skill. Verbal tests have the opposite fault so the best way and the usual way is to have tests of both sorts of skill. This leaves the difficulty of dealing with subjects where there is no suitable test in their own language or with those whose cultural background involves what might be called verbal deprivation. We must do what we can to remedy these defects. However, we have to beware of what I call 'But-what-about?-ism'. There is an absurd concept of morality which says that no good thing shall be done for anyone unless it can be done for everyone. Because, sadly, there are people with no legs, we do not forbid dancing.

I say that a group test of intelligence will reveal some but not all of the very bright children who can be helped with more suitable educational courses. Immediately these kind hearted moralists will say 'but what about the others'? It would be easy to show that no human advance of any kind would be possible if this version of morality were strictly followed. The proper answer to 'what about?' questions can only be 'Benefit as many as possible and never forget those you cannot'. It must never be 'perfection or nothing, everyone or no one' so that no hidden talents are discovered and helped for the general benefit. Surely it is *immoral* to deprive society of the optimum contribution from one child because another unknown child's potential contribution may have been lost because your method is imperfect.

Are mental differences inherited?

I now have another vexed question to get out of the way, the question of the heritability of differences in intelligence.

It was once taken for granted in a simple way that children tended to take after their parents in many ways. The modern science of genetics can now explain in detail exactly how this happens. It can explain both the heritability of parental traits and the random shuffling process by which, as it were, the two genetic packs of cards (or genes), one from each parent, are shuffled and re-matched by the crossover process. What a child inherits comes from both parents, but the particular hand he draws in the genetic lottery owes something to chance shuffling. If it were not for the politics of egalitarianism there would not be any public doubt about the fact that this applies with human intelligence as with innumerable other factors. Genetic theory tells that if the child's parents are bright then the chance that the child will be bright is raised, and if they are dull it is lowered. It also tells us to expect to find rare but significant exceptions where a bright pair produce a retarded child and vice versa. These predictions are closely fulfilled in practice and would normally be thought to confirm the view that heredity plays a part in differences of intelligence as it does with every other human difference. But no! It does not suit some kindly egalitarians to believe that Nature could be so unkind. Differences of intelligence are so much more important to mankind, especially in this advanced civilisation, that the idea that some are born with a built-in advantage in this vital respect is intolerable. So despite convincing evidence from many twin studies (besides those of Sir Cyril Burt, which some suspect) there are many gentle academic souls who are prepared to stake their academic and general reputation on declarations to the effect that differences of intelligence are unlike all the other differences and are completely unaffected by the genes. We can bear our differences in beauty, skill, sporting prowess, colour, height, weight, etc. Our differences in thinking power are intolerable.

The truth is fairly plain. Differences in intelligence, the general factor, have dual (or multiple) causes. They are probably largely determined by the genes. The difference in cleverness between a man and a dog is not environmental. Nor is the difference between a congenital idiot and a genius. But the difference in IQ or any other attempt to *measure* the underlying genetic characteristics are affected by the environment to a greater and lesser extent. The differences in manifest intelligence between normal children within a given culture seem to be around 70 per cent by the variability within the culture of the way they were brought up. This would be as accurate a way of looking at it as you are likely to get.

The influence of the home

It is certainly true that manifest intelligence or mental efficiency, ability to do well academically and make profitable use of the inborn potential is affected very much by the the way a child was brought up, especially during the magic first five years. This has caused Professor Wall to proclaim that, academically a child is made or lost before it gets to school. He tested the examination results of children matched for IQ but from different social backgrounds. He found that over large samples those from homes where the parents were positive towards study and learning, where there were books around and intelligent discussion, had a strong tendency to produce more academic high flyers than those where these things were absent. This is the most important lesson for the parents of a brilliant child and I shall deal with the matter at greater length later.

As Dr Jack Cohen reminds us in *The Privileged Ape*, (Parthenon Publications), there are two kinds of heredity in human social groups. The genetic heredity determines the physical characteristic of each individual and their general intelligence among many other traits.

The second thing every child inherits is the information-base, the lifestyle skills and know-how of the cultural grouping in which it is brought up. Cohen calls this investment from one generation into the next 'privilege' in various forms. He shows clearly that the advanced life forms invest more 'privilege' in succeeding generations than the primitive ones. Mankind is at the top of this 'investment in the young' tree with young who remain immature and dependent on inherited 'privilege' for a quarter of their life term, a period of 16 years. This may clash with our social ideas of 'justice' or 'fairness', but it is the way things are and the way humanity is and got where it is.

Are selection and ranking divisive?

Chambers' Dictionary defines divisive as 'forming divisions or separations'. Well, of course, selection is divisive if that is what is meant, but so are many kind of school classes, office or factory departments such as are unavoidable in any social organisation whatever. I assume that the meaning of the word in the context of education is that a divisive system is one which sets one division against another in some sort of conflict. If it does not mean that it is an absurd truism. (If you separate groups they will be separate.)

Now one of the tools that teachers used to employ to improve learning motivation in a class was the ranking system by which every child sat at a place which showed his scholastic success. The most studious and successful at the back and the 'bottom of the class' under teacher's eye in the front row. This is extremely unfashionable now and is said to be very harmful indeed. Questioning children, I have discovered that if the teacher does not rank the children they rank themselves (though not in the same way). There was also another kind of division, slow learning unmotivated children were taught in separate classses from fast learning studious ones.

My observation at school and as a department head, then Works Manager, then Managing Director in industry, is that similar ranking is universal and self-generating in any stable functioning group. What I found was that there were many little disputes and quarrels in any new group until this 'pecking order' type ranking established itself from the mutual interaction of the group members. After that I found that what caused conflict was any threat or challenge to the established pecking order, not the order itself. The only strike threats I ever had seemed to be aimed at preserving these inequalities of status, influence, and reward. Preserving differentials rather than abolishing them was always the popular thrust.

Similarly, the broader class rankings seem to establish themselves spontaneously. The management in the firm which I saw develop from small beginnings, insisted at first on an all-in-together system with no main divisions. But it soon emerged that different sorts of workers classified themselves. They preferred to sit together and eat together and were not comfortable with a wide social mix. The re-emergence of the normal class divisions took many years and was strongly resisted at the top level but it ended with more levels than is normal and I can say for sure that the pressure came from the self-ranked lower ranks.

The only clue to this mystery that suggests itself is the fact that many social vertebrates (backboned animals that live together co-operatively) have a similar social arrangement; social groups of fishes, birds and mammals, tend to develop the pecking order that was first noticed by ethnologists observing chickens. It seems to me to be rather a means of social stability than the reverse.

If influence, status and priorities in any group are always in contention, always provisional, unsettled, it would create more quarrelsome division than if they are, after a trial period finally resolved, *no matter how.* My conclusion is that far from being divisive in the sense of promoting instability and conflict, these natural spontaneous rankings and divisions have exactly the reverse effect. They are a necessary condition of stable, efficient and effective social groups. Divisiveness in the negative sense is no argument against educational selection or ranking.

What Terman showed

For many years there has been a campaign to discredit the intelligence test as a diagnostic tool which can help a teacher to do the vital job they have taken on, that of educating every child to the limit of its willingness and ability. Left wing intellectuals were so intoxicated by the attractive idea that people are all born alike not only in rights but in ability that they have attacked any art which reveals the rich diversity of humanity as biased and unfair. The character assassination of Sir Cyril Burt, which has been so thoroughly exposed by Professor Ronald Fletcher, was one example of how far people were prepared to go to kill any opposition to the idea that people are as alike as clone mates at birth and that all differences arise from 'unfair social inequalities'.

Those who still entertain doubts about the diagnostic value of the intelligence test should consider the remarkable longitudinal study carried out by Professor Lewis Terman. He selected 1,500 children on IQ tests in the '20s. There was also a control group of 1,500 children randomly chosen at the same time. Both groups were followed regularly and their performance checked and recorded. The results were unequivocal. They showed quite clearly that potential ability can be discovered very early. It also showed that if it is discovered and fostered it can flourish and make a contribution to the general welfare. The selected boys and girls both, on average, went on to do more years of education. In these days before the women's movement most of the girls did not go on into professional life but the 800 boys' careers showed clearly that the IQ test results were predictive.

It was not just that they were good scholars or that they did far better in academic qualifications. They excelled in every way.

By the time the gifted group had reached the age of 40 the men had published 67 books, 1,400 scientific or technical articles, over 200 novels or short stories, and patented many inventions. Generally speaking the gifted group did better than the controls in every possible way. However, there were exceptions other than the women.

This shows that it is true that ability needs to be fostered if it is to be revealed. It revealed an enormous waste of the potential ability of the girls and the fact that, once revealed, the boys chosen early for a high IQ score excelled in every possible way compared with the control group. The girls were discovered, but their gifts were not fostered, their ambitions were not roused to most career options and thus their gifts were limited. So much for the claim that there is no need to worry about the clever ones, that they are bound to make their own way! An able child needs to have a mentor who will recognise its promise and encourage its fulfilment.

(Terman 1925; Terman and Oden, 1947, 1959; Sears and Barbee, 1977: Goleman, 1980.)

The lesson is this. First of all, parents and teachers need to know. Second they must, carefully and temperately, inspire, challenge and motivate their promising children. They must set and raise targets and ambitions. The surest way to fail in this is not to try, the second surest is to try too hard.

Chapter 2

Bringing up a bright child – good news, bad news

FOR THE PARENT of a very intelligent child I have good news and bad news. I think it fair that you should be warned before you attempt a first approximate assessment of your child's general ability as you are invited to do in this chapter. Maybe, after my warnings and promises, you will not want to know. I hope you *do* want to know. If you find out that you have an exceptionally intelligent child these will be your problems.

Let us start with the bad news. I assume that you, the parent reader, are a responsible citizen and loving parent. I also assume that you suspect that your child is not comfortably about or just above average but truly a high flyer. In that case you have been landed with a very considerable and difficult social responsibility; a prolonged and difficult task. Your child is very important to the First World society you live in because it has the potential, as an adult, of contributing much more to the common welfare than most other children. As a responsible citizen and as a parent you will feel it your duty to maximise that potential. And that will make demands upon you beyond those which other citizens support. To make the most of your child as an individual and as a social contributor you may feel you ought to encourage your child to make demands upon itself beyond what is normal. This should never be done without the child's own best interests at heart. Especially it should never be done without the child's willing consent. Your child must never be used as a vehicle for your own disappointed aspirations. This is vital. But you must be even more careful not to set any limit to the child's *own* reasonable ambitions. I judge this to be the most frequent injustice.

Higher education, as I have said, is often looked upon as a privilege for the lucky few, but your child will find that it is a period of very hard, unpaid work at subsistence maintenance. This is what we expect of the intelligent and studious child. You might find yourself persuading your child that it is in its interest to defer joining the working world of rewards and status for many years in the hope that it will qualify for much more demanding roles of much greater responsibility and a greater work load later on. There may be rewards in money, honour and status but they are not certain and will have to be earned. You might also have to struggle with the social and educational authorities to get the unusual, specialist, advanced teaching which your unusual child needs if it is to fill the demanding roles mentioned. And for all this you will get no gratitude or thanks (except perhaps from the child in later life). What you will get from neighbours and other parents is envy. From hard-pressed and sometimes egalitarian educational authorities, you will get the brush-off, unless you are lucky or persistent. More will depend on you the parent than on anyone else. The parental influence has been shown in hard statistics to be crucial.

In addition you will have a lively, curious, demanding, often adventurous and perhaps mischievous child who will ask a million difficult questions and pose a thousand unusual problems. Your child will be the precious bane and the glory of your life.

Now comes the good news. After its long, unpaid education your child may do well and be well rewarded in money and status for its extra education, training, hard work and responsibility.

You will have a lively, stimulating, interesting, capable recruit to your family of which you can be tacitly proud. Home life will be absorbing, often exasperating, but vital. You will never be bored. And if things go fairly well you will have, over a long period, one of the most joyous and deeply satisfying emotional experiences that it is given to any man or woman on this planet to have. You will have the wonder and fulfilment of loving, watching, helping and guiding the development of the most important and wonderful thing in the universe of which mankind is sensible, a well brought up, well educated young man or woman of very high potential for service and self expression.

You will have the happiness of knowing that you have served your family and your nation in an exemplary fashion and contributed more than your fair share to the common weal. You will have played a part in making the universe safer for living intelligence. In your later years, you will be entitled to feel some modest pride in your unacknowledged and unrecognised contribution to your own culture, to this World Culture and civilisation, and maybe to humanity in general.

How do you find out if your child is exceptional? Loving parents with little experience of the full range of difference in children can easily be deceived. They may take the superior as normal or vice versa. To know the superior we have to know the average.

An exemplary children's IQ test is given below but children cannot be formally tested until they are six (or at least have a mental age of six, which can happen with some children as young as three and a half). Even then the results are none too reliable, especially bad results.

Before the age of six we shall have to rely on watching the progress of the baby and trying to judge its advancement along the scale of normal development. There follows such a scale. Beyond that is the first approximation IQ test for normal children over six but a bright child of five should be able to register a score. Very exceptional children as young as three and a half *might* be able to do it.

How to spot a bright baby

First an important caveat about the first approximation guides and tests offered here. What I say applies to some extent to all intelligence tests. They must be taken seriously but not too seriously. The accepted view, much emphasised by professional psychologists, is that the only really valid intelligence test is an individual test administered by an qualified educational psychologist.

Further, tests administered by untrained persons are less reliable but experience in Mensa shows that a majority of the self- or parent-administered tests can give a reasonably close first approximation for the very gifted child or adult. But there can be the occasional gross error, so do not let your expectation be unduly raised or lowered. Providing the parent is not foolishly 'helping the child' so as to deceive himself, errors of over estimation are quite rare. The greatest risk is that of missing potential, so if your child does very much worse than you expected you should consider the advisability of an individual professional test. An important point with young children especially is motivation. There is an assumption behind every intelligence test. It is assumed that the subject is trying. If there is no motivation to succeed then the test tells us little or nothing. The professional will be able to assess this factor and has ways of overcoming lack of motivation.

Group tests under a trained expert are better than home tests but they too are less reliable than individual tests by qualified psychologists.

There are some general observations which teachers and parents are advised to watch for and these can be summed up in a few sentences. If these primary indications are favourable then it is as well to look through the more detailed method given below in the Development-Age Table for Babies.

The first and most important thing to remember is that the brighter a child is the more different it is from other children. The second thing is that the brighter a child is the more different it is from *other bright children*. They get more variable as they get brighter. That is the challenge and the stimulus for those who try to help them. There is not a *single* problem of bright children, there are *numerous* problems of bright children, all different. Here are some general points concerning promising babies:

1 They are usually forward in all development, their eyes focus early and they are early to start following movement of large objects with their eyes.

2 They are usually more energetic, active and adventurous than other children. Sometimes they seem to need less sleep.

3 They learn quickly and soon show that they understand the daily routine. They show pleasurable and negative *anticipation* early in life.

4 They are unusually curious and inquisitive. They get interested by

new toys and are quickly bored with toys that they have mastered. They love picture books and soon learn to turn the pages.

5 They are quick to understand instructions, often long before they can say the words that show they can understand them.

6 They are early to show that they know when they are going against the rules. They are cautious and watch the parents when they start to be naughty.

7 They talk early and soon develop a spoken and an understood vocabulary much greater than usual for a given age. Their pronunciation is better with less childish errors. These verbal indications are the most important.

8 They are often, but not always, early to crawl and walk and pass the other stages of motor learning. But slow motor learning is *not* a bad intellectual sign.

9 They soon become autonomous (self-willed). They know what they like and want and are not easily over-persuaded.

10 They show a longer than usual attention span. They are more persistent and less easily distracted than average babies of the age.

Development stages for babies

As I have said, the younger the child the more difficult to predict future intelligence, but there are early signs by which some really bright children can be spotted. Precocity – early learning – is a reliable positive sign, but the absence of it is not necessarily a negative one. There is no truth in the popular myth that precocious children tend to 'burn out', or relapse. If a baby performs beyond its age level in the stages which follow you would be wise to be prepared to provide for a bright, forward child as it grows up.

What follows is a summary and consensus of a number of accounts of the cognitive development of what is classed as a normal child, that is a child of average IQ, ie, 100.

Dr Arnold Gesell is the pioneer of this method and Drs Richard Lansdown and Mary Sheridan have developed and extended these methods. It is not claimed that these stages are based on a thorough statistical examination of a really large random sample, but they are modelled on similar scales which have been used by many skilled paediatricians and clinicians with success for a long time. Parents should use them with caution and without anxiety or tension. The table should be consulted purely for the purpose of observation and reference, not to conduct a test on the baby. Parents should consult their doctor if they find the outcome is very much unexpected in any way. It is just possible they may reveal clinical conditions, eg, sight, hearing or motor defects.

They also tell parents whether the child has advanced as far as the average in cognitive skills at any age and also whether it is beyond the average with a feeling as to how much beyond. There are great variations between children and this is quite normal. You will know that a child has reached a particular stage when it can perform about three quarters of the tasks for its age. If it can perform most of the tasks for any younger age and about a quarter of the tasks of the next age given, then it may be considered advanced. For instance if a child of two could, on the language and adaption tests, perform almost as well as a $2\frac{1}{2}$ year old and complete some of the tests for a three year old it would be safe to say that it was advanced six months, which rather vaguely predicts an IQ of 125 (IQ = $100 \times 2.5/2.0 = 125$).

One more thing has to be explained. We have to divide the baby's performance into two distinct and separate categories for our present purpose, spotting the clever child early.

The intelligent child is advanced in the whole set of abilities that are called 'cognitive'. They are basically social skills, not motor or movement skills. They are to do with comprehension of social situations which are describable in symbolic ways, words or diagrams. Every child has to learn to control and use its body like any young animal, it also has to learn social relations and communication with other people. The two sorts of learning are quite different and are not closely related. What we are concerned with in this book is not bodily skills or agility but social and communication skills, those where the word 'intelligence' applies. Usually a cognitively advanced child makes little better than average progress at purely 'motor' learning, using its muscular system skilfully. It may even be slower at purely motor learning. For instance it often understands many words and sentences that it cannot yet say. One of the problems we have to watch for in cognitively advanced children is this unevenness of development.

Gesell found it convenient to classify early learning into four categories

1 Motor Body skills, handling, walking.

2 Personal social Personal relations, play, toilet skills..

3 Language Verbal comprehension, speech, sentences.

4 Adaptive Using body skills purposively or in play.

Of these the last two most reflect intelligence in the sense of cognitive ability although it can be seen in some aspects of **2**.

It is therefore the sections **3** and **4**, the language and adaptive sections, that should be especially looked at to check for cognitive advancement.

The Development-Age Table for babies
One month

1 Motor
Limbs move jerkily almost at random. Turns towards touch on cheek. No head control. Hands unusually clenched. Stiffens legs if held erect on feet.

2 Personal social
Sleeps a lot. Sucks. Stops crying when lifted. Grasps if palm touched. (Smiling after 6 weeks.)

3 Language
Startles at loud noises, may cry. Freezes on hearing unusual sound. Stops whimpering for reassuring human voice.

4 Adaptive
Stares at wall or window. Follows very close moving objects with eyes. Watches mother's face when she is close.

Three months

1 Motor
Limbs less stiff, they move more easily and continuously. Hands less clenched. Strong kicking. Holds head erect for a while when upright.

2 Personal social
Smiles and recognises feeding and bath time. Stares at mother's face while feeding. Responds with pleasure to fondling and tickling. Can hold things briefly but does not watch them as it does so.

3 Language
Cries, turns away from loud unusual noises. Quietens and smiles to mother's voice or other steady sounds. Is excited by approaching footsteps, bath sounds, etc. Turns eyes towards sounds. Crows and gurgles when pleased.

4 Adaptive
Stares at things and takes an interest in them, especially faces. Can be seen to be looking around to see things it hears. Follows nearby movements with eyes. Watches own hands and clasps them. Is expectantly excited at feeding time.

Six months

1 Motor
Can lift head from pillow. Unsupported sitting with turning to look around. Pulls self upright. Puts up hands to be lifted. Moves arms and legs purposefully, kicks strongly. Rolls over. Head erect when sitting.

2 Personal social
Is interested in its foot movements. Can reach for and grasp small toys two handed. Gnaws at everything it grasps. Shakes and watches rattle purposively. Usually friendly with strangers but sometimes silent or anxious and shy.

3 Language
Turns to mother's voice. Makes random noises, long vowels but some syllables, eg, 'bee', 'doe', 'goo'. Laughs, chuckles, screams. Responds to mother's voice tones.

4 Adaptive
Very inquisitive about things close by. Watches everything close to it but makes only vague searching movements when things go out of sight. Eyes move together. Uses whole hand in grasping.

Nine months

1 Motor
Can sit alone for a time. Rolls or wriggles to move body, tries to crawl. Very active in pram. Can stand for a while when holding. Cannot lower self. Makes stepping movements when held standing.

2 Personal social
Holds cups and spoons, licks them. Holds and chews biscuits. Stiffens when annoyed. Distinguishes strangers from family. Needs reassurance with strangers and hides face and clings to known person. Holds out toy to others but does not let go.

3 Language
Makes noises to attract attention and inform. Shouts then listens in turn. Babbles a lot but no words. Tries to imitate sounds but not words. Understands one or two words such as 'No'.

4 Adaptive
Picks up small things easily. Drops toys for fun. Follows toys that roll out of sight with eyes. Handles objects confidently from hand to hand, examining all sides. Watches the activities of people around with close interest for a few seconds.

Twelve months

1 Motor
Sits securely, can sit up from lying down. Fast crawling, can stand, holding on and let self down again. Sidles around furniture holding on, can walk with helping hand. Stands alone for a moment or two.

2 Personal social
Can drink from cup with help and hold but not quite use spoon. Stops drooling and stops gnawing any object. Can put small objects into a container and take them out again. Will give things to adults when asked or at own will. Likes company all the time. Imitates 'bye bye' and clapping. Shows affection to those it knows.

3 Language
Responds to own name. Shows that it knows several usual words. Obeys simple commands, 'Come to Daddy', 'Give it to Mummy'. Babbles loudly and continuously and is better at imitating simple sounds.

4 Adaptive
Points at what it wants and follows movement of a toy across a room. Follows moving objects out of doors intently.

Fifteen months

1 Motor
Walks carefully with feet wide apart and arms up to balance with. Bumps into things and falls or squats with a bump. Can stand up without help. Can kneel by itself. Can crawl upstairs.

2 Personal social

Complains of wet nappy. Can hold give and take a cup. Helps its mother to dress it. Can hold but not quite manage spoon. Restless and curious. A few tantrums. Needs a lot of supervision because it is more adventurously exploratory. Can push a toy pram or animal on wheels. Is always throwing things down. Insists on adults' presence and attention.

3 Language

Speaks up to six or seven recognisable words and understands many. Much jabbering with a greater range of sounds and inflections. Can point out familiar things and people when asked. Obeys simple commands, eg, 'Shut the door', 'Get your hat'.

4 Adaptive

Can scribble with crayon, pick up string, crumbs, accurately. Can pile two bricks. Looks out of the window at what is going on. Points demandingly at what it wants. Is interested in pictures in books. Can follow a thrown object with its eyes.

Eighteen months

1 Motor

Walks with feet closer together, starts, stops without stumbling. Runs watching ground close ahead, has trouble with obstacles. Pushes large objects and wheeled toys around or carries a large teddy. Climbs into adult chair frontwards before turning and sitting. With help can climb stairs upright. Picks things from floor from standing. Comes down stairs on bottom.

2 Personal social

Can drink from mug with two hands and pass cup back. Can just get food to mouth on spoon. Very exploratory and curious. Calls for potty and is clean. Can take off clothes, shoes, etc. Gnawing toys is finished. Less throwing down. Begins to contradict and be naughty but also seeks assurance. If adult near plays alone.

3 Language

Gabbling and jabbering continue but up to 20 spoken words. Tries to sing, likes stories and rhymes. Repeats important words in sentence spoken to it. Can point to limbs and features on a person or doll when they are named.

4 Adaptive

Can pile three bricks, scribble on paper, pick up fine particles and enjoy picture books and stories, turning several pages at a time. Points to distant objects outdoors when interested.

Two years

1 Motor

Squats and rises without using hands. Tows corded toy. Climbs up and down on chair to look out of window. Can throw without falling but not quite kick a ball. Climbs stairs holding bannister.

2 Personal social
Uses cup and spoon perfectly. Dresses self, shoes hat etc. Potty trained during day. Can open doors and runs into garden. Copies housework. Strong sense of possession. Will not share. Has tantrums but can be pacified easily. Pretence games start. Tolerates other children but no mutual play yet.

3 Language
Uses up to 50 words and can use two or three words together. Names self. Talks to self a lot. Repeats words and phrases it hears. Asks the name of things. Points to and says names of things like eyes, nose, hands, head.

4 Adaptive
Is now either left- or right-handed. Names familiar people in photographs. Can pile six bricks. Enjoys picture books and name details in drawings. Can draw a vertical line, a circular scribble and dots. Names what is represented by small toys.

Two and a half years

1 Motor
Can run, jump, climb and kick a large ball quite well. Can push large toys around but not too good at getting around obstructions. Can walk up stairs alone but uses banister coming down.

2 Personal social
Can pull down trousers or knickers for toilet but not get them up again. Eating OK with spoon or fork. Active and often naughty and defiant but very dependent emotionally on adults. No night bed-wetting if picked up. Long pretence play sessions with adult consulted. Interested in other children's play but joins only briefly. Not ready for sharing yet.

3 Language
Up to 200 hundred words are spoken and many more understood. Pronunciation still childish. Child still repeats words and phrases from what it hears, just to practise. Lots of What? Where? Why? questions. Uses 'I', 'we', 'you' correctly. Knows names in full and talks to self a lot, understandably.

4 Adaptive
Can stack seven or eight bricks and pick up tiny objects with one eye covered. Spots and names small details in books and can draw lines, circles, T, V and similar simple letters, can spot self in photographs.

Three years

1 Motor
Can stand on one foot briefly, walk on tip-toe and sit with feet crossed. Rides tricycle, climbs well, runs and swerves and dodges well, even when pushing wheeled toys. Steps upstairs but usually jumps down.

2 Personal social
Can wash hands and face. No bed-wetting. Can manage in the toilet with help with buttons. Not so naughty and wilful, more loving. Begins to help

in the house and garden. Plenty of imaginative pretence in play with invented objects and people. Likes to play with bricks and other floor toys. Plays with other children and shares things with them. Cuddles younger children.

3 Language
Now knows many words but pronunciation still childish. Can give name and sex. Talks to self a lot about what has happened and some pretend stories. Can converse in a connected way. Lots of questions and a love of stories repeated many times. Can recite simple poems and rhymes.

4 Adaptive
Can pick up pin or thread with one eye covered. Builds tower of 9 bricks. Can draw a man with a head and perhaps more detail. Can use scissors and a paint brush on a large board.

Four years

1 Motor
Climbs stairs normally. Runs on toes. Climbs trees. Hops. Good on tricycle. Can stand on one foot for 5 seconds. Can play with toys on the floor while standing.

2 Personal social
Can perform toilet, wash hands and clean teeth. Dressing and undressing OK with a little help. Self-willed and rude when thwarted. Takes turns in play. Likes joint play but switches between aggression and co-operation. Shows sympathy and concern for younger children when appropriate. Make believe and dressing up, builds constructions in garden.

3 Language
Speech better with fewer infant pronunciations. Describes recent happenings. Very curious about the meanings of words and full of all sorts of questions. Likes to be read to or told stories. Tells long tales sometimes.

4 Adaptive
Matches four simple colours correctly. Draws recognisable man with all the essential features. Can copy an H, a T, and a cross. Can copy a simple construction of 9 or 10 bricks.

Five years

1 Motor
Can dance to music, climb, hop, slide, swing, dig, vigorously and well. Stands on one foot for 8 seconds. Strong grip both hands.

2 Personal social
Uses knife and fork well. Washes self with a little supervision. Behaviour begins to be sensible and autonomous. Dressing and undressing without help or instruction. Chooses friends. Games get more complex. Plans constructions better. Co-operative in play and accepts need for rules. Has a sense of time. Considerate to younger ones.

3 Language
Speech unhesitating and much better but some difficulty with a few sounds. Fond of stories, begins to be curious about abstract ideas. Knows birthday. Can define some words.

4 Adaptive
Can copy simple forms, square, triangle, etc. Can write about ten letters. Can produce simple recognisable drawings of familiar things. Can count up to 10 and name four colours.

Guide for parents of bright babies

Once you suspect that the baby is forward in learning you will want to know what care and attention it will need other than that which all babies need. Below I give an account of the consensus which arises from wide experience with thousands of bright people in Mensa and their children, from gifted children's organisations in many countries and all the literature about bright children that I have read over many years of intense interest in the subject.

This is the advice to parents:

Spend a lot of time with them
All babies do best if they have the close personal attention of one person for most of its time during the first few years. The child's mother is usually the best bet to provide this care because of the very close and special bonding that usually forms after birth. Too often that ideal is not realisable. There may be other children or the mother may need to work away from home.

Everyone nowadays accepts that some unusual children, those that are handicapped or retarded, need and must have more time, care and attention than the average. I have to say here that another kind of unusual children, promising or precocious ones, also need more time, care and attention. The first five years are by a long way the most important in any baby's life but in the life of a supernormal child this is even more so. More harm can be done to and more opportunities lost by a very promising child than by an average child if it fails to get the constant early interaction with and stimulation from that special mother-baby relationship, the closest and most intimate relationship of which we know. This is why I spoke above of the burden a bright child can be. To the person who takes the mother role it is often a great burden but usually a great delight as well.

Love them
Every new born baby needs love and cuddles. It has been swaddled as it were, in a secure, warm, moving but dark comfort for many months. The new world of sight and loud noises is harsh and startling. After each ration of experience of the strange outside world it needs a period wrapped in warmth with stirring motion, near a beating heart, and breathing lungs

with muffled, soothing speech and other body noises. Cuddling, rocking, swaddling, crooning, all these are womb substitute actions to reassure a baby. And of course the small baby which is going to turn out to be a bright child needs this as much as any other, and will be handicapped without it.

Stimulate them

Every child also needs stimulus if it is to learn to live in the world and mothering and fathering is the art of applying this in a balanced rational way, neither too much, nor too soon, nor too little, nor too late. And here we must say that right from birth the bright child needs more stimulus, more experience than other children to keep it interested.

During the brief periods of wakening, hang something bright and moving above cot or pram, and change it for something novel from time to time. Talk to the child all the time, it cannot hear too much of adult voices. It is best not to stop talking and tip-toe around when the baby sleeps, it will sleep through any familiar noise. If you start by hushing the whole family while baby is asleep it will need that hush to sleep at all. If you continue as normal it will be reassured by the noise rather than startled by it.

Give them a variety of toys

It is no problem nowadays to find a great range of toys suitable for every age rising by months. It is natural for all babies, especially bright ones, to get bored with a toy once they have mastered it. You have to keep them coming and gradually take away those which have done their job. But when the child gets really attached to one toy it is for reassurance and there is no need to remove it until it is rejected or neglected.

The way we learn is by trial and error. The great art of parenthood is to allow the child the right ration of each of these. No error, no learning. The child, especially the forward one, should always be pushing against its limits and that includes the limits set by the parent for its own safety. The limits have to be revised continually as the baby becomes more competent. A baby has an enormous lot to learn in a very short time and if it does not have a great urge to gain experience it has no chance. You must patiently allow it to explore its world and not be too quick to put out the helping hand. Sometimes when it calls for help you must hold off and insist on another try. But you must always signal and salute progress and success, raising the targets judiciously all the time.

The right program of teaching is to give the infant a balanced ration of success and failure so as to keep it interested and active but not bored by repetition. But do not insist on too many trys too early so as to get the 'Cannot do it,' or 'Mummy do it' response too often. Fight the urge to help too soon or often.

Talk to them

The very bright child needs adult conversation much more than other children, if it is to develop optimally (simple sentences but no baby talk).

Several statistical studies such as that by Dr J W B Douglas, show un-equivocally that only children and first children perform better in later life in entry to higher education, examination results and other 'success' signs like entries in *Who's Who*. The next advantaged group is *last* children, which seems to argue against a genetic explanation. A very likely causal factor is that parents pay more attention and spend more time talking to a first child or a last child. Also these children learn speech from adults or older children rather than from younger ones. Confirmation comes from the statistically established fact that children's speech development often tends to regress when they first go to school and mix more with other children. The advice I have to give here is this: bright children, more than most, need adult attention, talk, stories, chat, and to be read to interac-tively, with encouragement to interrupt, discuss and question. They need a lot of it. Modern life makes this advice difficult to follow in a hard-pressed two-job family but it is important to do what you can. For instance, intelligent, educated and chatty au pairs and baby sitters who speak clearly are to be preferred to others. Further the parent must put aside preconcep-tions about what level of discussion is suitable at any age. It is best to talk in a style as close to your normal adult style as you can without incompre-hension. You can often be surprised at how advanced a conversation with a child can be once the experiment is made.

Avoid baby talk

Do not make the mistake of encouraging baby talk by introducing it or even copying it from the child. Baby talk and immature pronunciation spreads among children. That is bad. Adults should not encourage it, even if it seems 'natural' and 'charming'. It is perfectly possible for a baby to learn correct pronunciation right from the start. I have seen this in my own children and grandchildren. My granddaughter, Alexandra, at 18 months could say several hundred words, many with several syllables. She makes few errors of pronunciation. She does meet other children but talks incessantly with her parents.

Can babies, should babies, be taught to read?

Another myth is spread by some teachers. The myth is that it is harmful for parents to teach children to read.

Many British teachers seem to have been trained to discourage parents even from letting the eager, curious child teach itself. 'That is our job', they say, insisting that anything the parents do to open the world of knowledge to a child by making it literate will handicap the child and teacher because the child will not be taught 'the proper way', usually meaning whatever way is the latest passing fad or fashion at a particular school.

The facts are these. They are well known in Mensa. Many children learn to read quite well long before they get to school. Many children become curious and teach themselves, others need very little encouragement. Quite often by the time they are four, three sometimes, they can read very well.

Others, Dr Rhodes Boyson estimates 10 per cent, spend 10 years, maybe 10 or 12,000 hours at school and remain functionally illiterate. I have met hundreds of Mensa members who claim to have been self-taught precocious readers and I have heard of no evidence of any harm that has resulted from such early reading. I have met none who has regretted it. Dr Margaret Pollak, a paediatrician at Kings College Hospital, describes the view that only professional teachers can teach reading as absolute nonsense. She advises parents to familiarise babies with letters and numbers as soon as they show any interest in them. There is absolutely no danger, nothing to be lost by constantly exposing an interested child to the experience of written forms and pictures and letting the child learn at its own pace. Pushing the child unduly is another matter and should not be done, but as long as the child is interested and enjoys the game you can continue without qualms.

A program to teach toddlers to read?

How about setting out to teach a bright baby below 18 months to read? Well, a bright baby of this age can recognise and name very complex and highly variable forms, such as a chair, a table or a human face and there is no reason why it cannot learn to recognise the form of a word which is much less complicated and less variable.

In the field of electronic pattern recognition, where I have had professional interest, it is well known that this is so. Automatic printed character recognition is normal while facial recognition devices are still rare, slow and fallible. There is a problem though and the answer to it was found by Glen Doman, the author of *Teach Your Baby To Read*. A baby learns first to recognise large objects and only gradually becomes good at classifying small ones. The baby, he found, can soon learn to recognise the word 'mummy' and 'daddy' and many others if they are written large enough. He starts with the words written in letters 75mm (3in) high and found that two-year-olds could learn to recognise and name these as well as anything else when the name and the word were presented together sufficiently frequently.

Doman says that you can start with a two-year-old and to leave it later is to waste the few, precious early fast-learning years when the child's ability to acquire knowledge is maximal. He reminds us that in the three years between two and five a child can learn an entire language and, if it is exposed to them, several languages, as many as four or five. 'Do not waste those precious years which never come again', Doman urges. Parents should get the book and try the method, but I give below the flavour of the method as a critical appreciation.

My only point is that the method is, in essence based on the 'Look and Say' method by which the whole word rather than the assembly of letters is learned. This is thought at a later age to be better for slow learners than for promising children who like to be able to puzzle out new words from the sounds of the letters. However, if a baby has built up a vocabulary of the most common words by the age of three it can be introduced to the phonetic method at four or five. It will have the great advantage of knowing many words and thus get contextual clues.

Doman argues reasonably that the child has to proceed from the known to the unknown and the concrete to the abstract. So words associated with concrete *things* are easy to learn. But letters are much more abstract concepts. A three- or four-year- old child with a database of recognised basic words can more easily puzzle out new words phonetically as its reasoning power develops.

Doman's method calls for these key points:

Do not start unless the child is interested and stop *before* the child gets bored.

He gives detailed instructions about the flash cards that must be made or obtained. The letters are gradually reduced from 100mm high to 25mm high and less. Lower case letters are used not capitals. This is what we read most of the time.

The exposure of the cards and telling the child what they say is gradual and designed to avoid the main enemy, boredom. You have to introduce new words as fast as the child seems to need them to keep interested. Babies soon get tired of the familiar and have an enormous curious appetite for the novel. They have to be like that. They have a lot to learn in a very short time.

Doman says that children should first be taught to read what he calls 'self' words, those about its own body, because the learning process extends gradually out from the self, eg, 'hand', 'nose', 'mouth', 'shoulder'. The parent says 'hand', squeezes the child's hand, exposes the 'hand' flash card, says 'this is a hand' shows the flash card and says it again. Previously learned words are constantly reviewed. When a few dozen words have been mastered the child goes on to learn words connected with the home. At a later stage sentence construction is tackled and so on.

Gradually, books with decreasing letter size and increasing vocabulary are introduced. The parent does not try to explain or define at the early stages, but relies on familiarity and repetition for the learning process. Tackle the alphabet at a late stage in the process when the child's ability at abstract reasoning is developing. Doman is most insistent that the whole process should be seen by the child as a happy game. There should be no tenseness or anxiety, just fun for both mother and child. This book is about bright children and it seems very likely that almost all such children would benefit if a parent, nurse or relative can find the time to teach reading from babyhood. I can assure the reader that it works.

How to spot a bright child

As with babies, I shall start with a general description of bright children over the age of five. Caveat. They are very different from each other, here are a few points they have in common.

Here are 20 points reprinted from the chapter on gifted children in my book *Check Your Child's IQ* Mensa Publications (1989). They come from a general consensus of those with experience in this field.

Highly intelligent children:

1 Possess superior powers of reasoning, of dealing with abstractions, of generalizing from specific facts, of understanding meanings, and of seeing into relationships.
2 Have great intellectual curiosity.
3 Learn easily and readily.
4 Have a wide range of interests.
5 Have a broad attention span that enables them to concentrate and persevere in solving problems and pursuing interests.
6 Are superior in the quantity and quality of vocabulary as compared with other children of their own age.
7 Have ability to do effective work independently.
8 Have learned to read early (often well before school age).
9 Exhibit keen powers of observation.
10 Show initiative and originality in intellectual work.
11 Show alertness and quick response to new ideas.
12 Are able to memorise quickly.
13 Have great interest in the nature of man and the universe (problems of origins and destiny, and so on).
14 Possess unusual imagination.
15 Follow complex directions easily.
16 Are rapid readers.
17 Have several hobbies.
18 Have reading interests that cover a wide range of subjects.
19 Make frequent and effective use of the library.
20 Are superior in mathematics, particularly in problem solving.

Obviously the first and most important step is to be sure that the child *is* bright. School progress is a satisfactory guide if it is good but an unreliable one if it is bad, for reasons which will appear. Either way it needs to be checked against an intelligence test.

However, a careful, conscientious parent can supervise a home test well enough to get a first approximation guesstimate as to where the child stands. So an IQ test is included below. It is important to carry out the instructions exactly. It is equally important not to take the results too seriously. If you carry out the instructions carefully and get a score much lower than you expected, do not worry, errors of underestimation are not infrequent. You might try a Mensa test or, better, get a properly supervised test by an educational psychologist. If you have been careful, not helped the child and you get a score much higher than expected, that is more likely to be an indication that you have been underestimating your child.

If you help the child by word, sign, hesitation or even by asking again when an error is made you will be deceiving no one but yourself.

Guesstimate IQ test for children aged 6 to 14

Parent's instructions

First find a time and place where you will not be interrupted for an hour. Make sure there are no other children, pets or other possible distractions present. The child should have a pencil sharpened at both ends and scribble paper to work things out on. Introduce the test as an interesting puzzle game or quiz. If you feel any tension the child will sense it, so do it when you and the child are relaxed. You may have to spend quite a time getting the child interested. Encourage the child to attempt each question but do not be too insistent. Encourage the child to guess, there is no penalty for wrong answers. Do not test more than one child at a time.

If the child can read the questions and understand them, let it do the test by itself, otherwise read out the questions and instructions slowly and clearly, making sure the child understands. Add nothing yourself. If the child asks questions just repeat the question slowly. Do not question a reply or say, 'Are you sure?' The child may change its mind but not after being prompted. Once the test starts note the time. The child should be encouraged to continue until it is clearly out of its depth and cannot do any more. In any case stop after exactly 45 minutes. If the child finishes the test before 45 minutes it may revise its earlier answers until the time is up.

Test instructions

Answer the questions carefully and quickly. Start at the beginning and go straight through to the end. The questions get harder as you go through. Hardly any child can do them all. There are no catches. If you underline too many answers that counts as wrong. You must not ask questions. You have 45 minutes.

NOW TURN OVER THE PAGE AND START THE TEST.

(Parent: place a sheet of blank paper over page 51 to conceal the answers). Note the time at the start of the test.)

The test

These are sums, adding and taking away. For example: Add 3 + 1 = 4
Take away 3 – 1 = 2
Now write down the answers to these sums. Some are take away –.
Some are add +

1	6 + 2 = ___	7	12 – 4 = ___	13	31 – 16 = ___
2	9 – 5 = ___	8	29 – 8 = ___	14	41 – 40 = ___
3	6 – 2 = ___	9	14 – 6 = ___	15	31 – 27 = ___
4	9 – 1 = ___	10	18 – 6 = ___	16	26 – 18 = ___
5	8 + 21 = ___	11	22 – 7 = ___	17	29 – 12 = ___
6	4 – 3 = ___	12	38 – 14 = ___		

Read these. There is a word left out. Underline (write a line under) the word from the line below that is best to go in the space.

Like this.

Example. John sleeps in his ___
table <u>bed</u> hat garden kitchen
<u>bed</u> is underlined because that is the best word.
Now you do it with the next ones. Underline the <u>best</u> word to go in the space.

18 Dogs ___ cats are pets.
    or and with hamsters budgies

19 John went ___ bed.
    at by to on over

20 ___ are built for people to live in.
    parks coats beds kennels houses

21 Apples are bigger ___ peas.
    than as by much on

22 A peach is a kind of ___
    skin bush vegetable fruit seed

23 Fishermen use nets to ___ fish.
    catch grab kill get have

24 John has ___ eyes.
    tall ten one two eyebrows

25 Steam ___ hot.
    makes is got has are

26 John stuck a ___ on a letter.
    writing address stamps stamp pillar-box

27 We use sugar to ___ our tea sweet.
    got cause have make made

28 Pencils are used to ___ with.
    write written right drawing writing

* * *

Here are some questions and some answers underneath. One answer is the best one. Underline the best answer.

29 What do we use to draw straight lines?
Rubber sponge ruler desk compasses

30 Where do we go to catch a train?
station stop street town road

31 What takes a road over a railway line?
crane junction path cutting bridge

32 What do we open when we are out in the rain?
penknife book umbrella sunshade comic

33 What do we call the joint between the foot and the leg?
knee elbow ankle thigh toes

34 What do we call the bottom of a shoe at the front?
heel leather plastic sole nails

35 What do we call the part of an apple where the pips are?
middle core seeds skin peel

36 What do we call a room full of shelves of books?
Shop kitchen library hall house

37 What is the middle of a wheel called?
hub axle pin rim tyre

38 What do we use to tie our shoes up?
string laces leather pins socks

39 Daisies, buttercups and tulips. What do we call them?
bunch flowers fruit seeds garden

40 What collects the rain-water as it comes off a roof?
road pipe gutter tap drain

41 What do you call the two holes in your nose?
bridge entrance nostrils lobes gaps

*   *   *

Read these words

dog <u>hat fat</u> mouse <u>mat</u> pot
Hat fat and <u>mat</u> are all underline because they <u>rhyme</u> they end with the same sound.

Now you do it. Read these lines of words. Underline the <u>THREE</u> words in each line which rhyme.

42 say sow too mow far low
43 pay pat say pot hut hay
44 monk drink bank chunk sunk tank
45 meant mint dent pat tent fate
46 late bright rite light mate court
47 teak take leek bake speak oak
48 peat late tight fate right weight
49 muff bough how tough grow puff

A B C D E F G H I J K L M N O P Q R S T U V W X Y Z

This is the Roman alphabet. Here are some questions about the order of the letters.

50 Which letter is midway between G and O? _____
51 Which letter is next but two after L? _____
52 Which letter is next but one before C? _____
53 Which letter is after the letter which comes after N? _____
54 Which letter is before the letter that comes before J? _____
55 Which letter is the fourth after the letter which is midway between J and P? _____
56 Which letter is next after the fifth letter after D? _____

Now imagine each letter is on a card that can be moved.

57 Now imagine the first two cards with letters on them are changed over. Then the second two are changed over, then the next two, and so on all through right up to Z. Which letter will now come sixteenth? _____
58 Now imagine the fourth card, the eighth, the twelfth the sixteenth and so on are taken away. What will now be the sixth letter? _____
59 What would now be the two middle letters? _____

*   *   *

Read these words.

long wide lengthy tall short strong
long and lengthy mean the same but short is the opposite so those words are underlined.

Now read each line of words and underline the two words that mean the same and the word that means the opposite of the other two.

60 start run jump begin finish walk
61 top end bottom side mountain summit
62 heavy weight weighty brilliant light feather
63 brilliant light lamp dim torch shining
64 come go approach farewell goodbye move
65 mute shouting music noisy deaf silent
66 growing contract climb shrink expand still
67 bliss smile misery grin anger joy
68 agreement quarrel meeting pact discussion deny
69 prosperous money impoverished millionaire affluent beggar
70 order arrange confusion combined muddle mixed

Here is a series of numbers. You have to find the <u>TWO</u> numbers that come next from the line below. You have to find the rule so that you can tell which are the right two numbers. Underline the right two numbers.

3 6 9 12 15 ? ?
1 9 <u>18</u> 4 3 <u>21</u>

<u>18</u> and <u>21</u> are underlined because they come next (the rule is add 3 each time).

That was easy. Now find the rule with these lines of numbers and underline the next two numbers from the list below.

71 1 6 2 6 3 ? ?
　　6 1 12 5 4 7

72 128 64 32 16 ? ?
　　10 12 4 3 8 9

73 2 5 4 7 6 ? ?
　　3 7 9 8 1 6

74 18 9 10 5 6 ? ?
　　3 9 6 2 1 4

75 3 4 6 7 9 ? ?
　　9 8 10 6 2 12

76 2 4 8 14 22 ? ?
　　32 3 7 15 44

77 2 3 30 31 310 ? ?
　　2143 3110 3454 311 4343 211

78 16 8 4 2 1 ? ?
　　$\frac{2}{3}$ $\frac{1}{2}$ $\frac{1}{8}$ $\frac{1}{4}$ $\frac{3}{4}$ 4

79 2 3 4 3 4 ? ?
　　3 5 10 4 2 1

*　*　*

Read this line.

Coal black (rain <u>snow</u> mine hat <u>white</u>)
Coal is black and snow is white so 'snow' and 'white' are underlined.

Now read this.

table-cloth table (floor hat <u>cup saucer</u> knife)
A table-cloth goes on a table so 'cup' and 'saucer' are underlined because a cup goes on a saucer.

Now underline the best <u>TWO</u> words in each line when you see the connection.

80 hen egg (cow cock rabbit honey milk)
81 scales weight (tape-measure length time thermometer volume)

49

82 skin man (cat chicken fish snake fur)
83 old wrinkled (smooth aged young happy father)
84 borrow lend (give snatch take have send)
85 lake pond (mountain hill sea land air)
86 cow herd (school house sheep cat child)

* * *

You have only ten pence pieces, twenty pence pieces and 50 pence pieces. A shop is selling marbles for 20 pence each and clay marbles for 15 pence each. You want to buy marbles spending just one coin and getting no change.

87 What is the most marbles you can buy for 50 pence? _____
88 How many can you get for 20 pence? _____
89 What is the smallest coin that will buy two sorts of marbles? _____
90 Using one coin to get the best value for your money will you buy clay or glass marbles? Underline which. clay glass.
91 You can spend any two coins. What is the most marbles you can get? _____

* * *

Now try these.

Jack is four and Joan is seven. Both their birthdays are today.

92 Some years ago Joan was twice as old as Jack. How many years? _____
93 One day Jack will be three quarters of Joan's age. In how many years will that be? _____
94 When Joan was four times as old as Jack, how old was he? _____
95 When Joan is three times as old as Jack is now, how old will he be? _____

* * *

A cube which measure 30cm each way is made up of a number of smaller cubes stuck together. They measure 10cm each way. The large cube is painted black on the top and the bottom. The sides are all painted white.

Answer these questions.

96 How many small cubes have no paint on them? _____
97 How many have black paint on them? _____
98 How many have white paint on them? _____
99 How many have both black and white paint on them? _____
100 How many are half painted? _____

THAT IS THE LAST QUESTION. YOU SHOULD SPEND THE REST OF THE TIME CHECKING ON YOUR ANSWERS TO MAKE SURE THAT YOU GET AS MANY AS POSSIBLE RIGHT. DO NOT TURN TO THE NEXT PAGE.

Marking the test

Here are the answers.

Each item is to be marked right or wrong, no credit for partial answers. One mark for each item that is correct.

No	Answer	No	Answer
1	8	40	gutter
2	4	41	nostrils
3	4	42	sow mow low
4	8	43	pay say hay
5	29	44	monk sunk chunk
6	1	45	meant dent tent
7	8	46	bright light rite
8	21	47	teak leek speak
9	8	48	late fate weight
10	12	49	muff tough puff
11	15	50	K
12	24	51	O
13	15	52	A
14	1	53	P
15	4	54	H
16	8	55	Q
17	17	56	J
18	and	57	O
19	to	58	G
20	houses	59	M N
21	than	60	start finish begin
22	fruit	61	top bottom summit
23	catch	62	heavy weighty light
24	two	63	brilliant dim shining
25	is	64	come go approach
26	stamp	65	silent noisy mute
27	make	66	contract shrink expand
28	write	67	bliss joy misery
29	ruler	68	quarrel pact agreement
30	station	69	prosperous affluent impoverished
31	bridge		
32	umbrella	70	muddle order confusion
33	ankle	71	6 4
34	sole	72	8 4
35	core	73	9 8
36	library	74	3 4
37	hub	75	10 12
38	laces	76	32 44
39	flower	77	311 3110

No	Answer		No	Answer
78	$\frac{1}{2}$ $\frac{1}{4}$		89	50 pence
79	5 4		90	glass
80	cow milk		91	6
81	tape-measure length		92	1
82	cat fur		93	5
83	young smooth		94	1
84	give take		95	9
85	mountain hill		96	1
86	child school		97	18
87	3		98	24
88	1		99	16
			100	8

How to work out your child's IQ from the score

First mark the test giving one mark for each question where the answer or answers are quite correct. Add up the correct answers (maximum 100). Look at the Key Number Table below. This gives a list of key numbers against each score. (The key number is 100 times the mental age in months for the score against it.)

1 Find the score nearest the child's score. Read off the key number opposite that score.

2 Calculate your child's age in months.

3 Divide the key number opposite the child's score by its age in months. Answer to the nearest whole number.

4 The answer is a rough guesstimate of the child's IQ.

5 If the number is over 175 take that as 175. The child has 'rung the bell'.

Example

A child age ten years and three months (123 months) scores 74.

The nearest score on the key table is 75 which gives a key number of 16900.

Divide this number by the child's age in months (123).

16900/123 = 134 to the nearest integer. This is the IQ of the child. It puts the child in the top tenth for intelligence. The average IQ is 100.

Key number table

Score	Key Number (mental age in months × 100)	Score	Key Number (mental age in months × 100)
5	6600	30	10100
10	7200	35	10700
15	7900	40	11300
20	8600	45	12000
25	9400	50	12800

Score	Key Number (mental age in months × 100)	Score	Key Number (mental age in months × 100)
55	13600	80	18000
60	14300	85	19100
65	15100	90	20300
70	15900	95+	21600
75	16900		

Myths about bright children

If you do find that you have a really bright child, there are a number of myths of which the parents of promising children have to be informed. Clearing away this deadwood of recent fashionable but unproven and even untested ideas is the first need.

In Britain there are a great deal of 'expert' opinions voiced and masses of unsupported and repetitive assertions made about the education of the gifted child. The overall tenor of most of these can be summed up by the sentence: 'Gifted children are no problem; they are lucky to be studious and clever and can very well look after themselves.'

But there has been astonishing little actual research on the important problem of making the best of the nation's rare talents. One of the few reported actual experiments in the provision of special courses was set up by Professor N R Tempest reported in his book *Teaching Clever Children 7-11*. He set up a class for selected high flyers at primary level and followed and researched the project for about four years. That was it, four years. Nevertheless many significant facts were revealed. The results of the research fly in the face of the complacent reassurances we often get from the above-mentioned experts.

Professor Tempest does not like the word 'gifted' in this context. He thinks it is too broad and too vague. The interest was in the one kind of giftedness that can be positively measured, diagnosed, early in life, general intelligence, cleverness, or intellectual giftedness. And by that he meant general forwardness in *all* learning abilities. His 'clever' child between seven and eleven years old could be between two and four years in front of the average child in education. He stresses that whether or not the clever child shows its ability depends on its circumstances. He says for instance 'occasionally a child may range four or more years beyond his grade level in measured achievement, yet give no indication of this. Since the child loves school and is eager to adapt himself to the new environment and to please his teacher, he actually may work hard to obscure any interests and abilities which are at variance with the classroom procedures.'

I have already mentioned the 'precocity burns out' myth. There is no truth in it. If you have a really bright child the advice you will get from many sides is not to 'overtax the child's brain', to 'drive it too hard'. This is unproven nonsense, not unclouded with envy. With a bright child you

53

will find that it is not you that is overtaxing and driving, you will be overtaxed and driven yourself, trying to keep up with a child who will be setting the pace and wearing you out. Normally you will find that you yourself are the limiting factor so that you have to do the best you can to keep up the progress, the interest, the challenge and the stimulation. The bright child is usually insatiably curious, energetic and untired and if they are not so, and you are sure you are right about how promising the child is, you should ask yourself whether the child has learned your own limits and is adjusting to a slower pace than is right for it.

This is where the idea of an uncle, aunt, grandparent or friend, an honorary relative or mentor may usefully be encouraged. Certainly the circle of friends and relatives who will interact creatively with the child should be enlarged as much as possible. (The mentor relationship which will be described in detail later has been shown to be an important factor where a child has later been found to develop its full potential).

While the child is interested and stimulated by such contacts there need be no fear that they are harming it. If a bright child is sent, for instance, to a kindergarten or play school it is right, if not essential, to choose one where its unusual needs will be met. Its greater appetite for stimulation, its vigorous curiosity and need for variety should and must be satisfied. Bright children are likely to be ready for interactive play with other children earlier than others. To bring them together with other children, especially others like themselves, for at least part of the time is good. There is a down side to this mentioned above. Children need to learn speech from adults not baby-talk from babies.

The contrary argument is often advanced. It is argued that it is harmful to bring a group of able children together to stimulate and interest each other. As mentioned previously, I have never seen the slightest evidence for this absurd idea. It is an ideological argument without the remotest justification. Those who advance it assume that all bright, studious children are from one social class and, insultingly, average and below ones from another. They think that the mixing of the different social class sub-cultures is a Good Thing which will somehow mitigate something called the Class War which, against the evidence, they insist is going on. Bright children, like retarded ones and all other kinds of children, have parents from all the social and occupational classes. The majority of the bright children in each generation always come from what are thought of as 'working class parents' for the simple reason that there are a lot more of them. Ideological social engineering should have no place in the important business of getting the best from and doing the best for the nation's students, let alone the high flyers among them. No venture, institution or industry could survive if, as well as all its other problems of fitting people comfortably and effectively into roles, it had to ensure a thorough social, occupational and income mix in all sections at all times.

Every child should get experience of the range of human ability and of the range of social and ethnic subcultures. This can be arranged in social, sporting, church, club meetings, and can happen in entertainment, play and friendships, but every child has a very special extra need in the classroom and during study. It needs to have the right balance of success and failure, the right level of competition and challenge. This must be neither too severe nor too easy. The high flyer especially needs to get what is difficult to provide, enough stimulus and competition so that it does not get too used to being always the outsider, the clever one. It needs friends and rivals of its own age (and thus its own stage of emotional development) which have reached a similar stage of cognitive maturity also. A bright child needs to come up against others like itself.

Another fallacy is the compensation myth mentioned earlier. It is widely believed that ability and advantage are distributed by the fates on a fair-shares basis. If nature gives you an advantage it is likely to make you pay for it with a compensatory disadvantage. It is supposed that very bright children are likely to be emotionally unstable or have other compensatory handicaps. This is an example of a statement that is not only untruthful but the reverse of the truth. As I said at the beginning of the book, and as has been completely established in a 40-year study by Professors Terman and Oden, a sample of gifted children seems to excel in many ways apparently not associated with their intelligence.

The compensation myth led to the false stereotype of the bright child who is a weedy, bespectacled swot who is no good at sport and tends to be weak, pimply and unlovely. Much as it suits human ideas of justice this is again the opposite of the truth. Bright children come in all sorts, have the full range of human variation on other ways of being different but, as Terman's monumental study has shown they tend, on the average, over large samples, to be taller, stronger, heavier, more athletic, more balanced emotionally and superior (as most of us would judge it) in many other ways. They even seem to be, if anything, happier. Nature is often unfair.

Should a bright child be told?

There are parents and teachers who cherish the illusion that children can and should be deceived about how intelligent they are. If a child mixes with other children it soon develops the power to judge them and once it spots that there are variables in height, strength and other traits it begins to spot the differences. It is not possible to convince a bright child that it is average or a dunce. It simply lowers the credibility of the teller. 'Know thyself', was always good advice and it is good for children to know their strengths and weaknesses. A bright child should feel that its higher intelligence raises the standards applied to it. It is best not to praise cleverness. But the effort put into solving problems and using gifts must be signalled and judiciously praised with carefully rising targets. Remember that easy praise is not valued by the intelligent child. The important reason why the child must know is to *maintain* modesty, to prevent the big-head syndrome. This is because the big-head syndrome has a price. It has to be paid for in popularity. Mental ability is a gift not a virtue. It is not praiseworthy to be given something. It is the story of the talents. It is not *having* them, it is what you *do* with them that counts. But a bright child needs confidence too. It needs to be encouraged to stand its ground when challenged. As it gets older it will sometimes be right when it is contradicted by those in authority. The lesson is to be persistent but to do so with temperance and tact. It is just at these moments that discriminating learning is happening.

Family rivalry

The bright child in an average family has, and causes, a problem. It is not so bad if it happens to be the oldest, but the senior child can be upset if a younger sib is too forward. The problem for the parent is to find ways of developing, encouraging and challenging the precocious one without giving the impression that it gets more love or attention than the others. The adjustment can be made by correctly setting the aspiration levels so that praise, blame and affection is equally shared between them all. It is no easy problem, especially when special educational provision for the bright one is justified and needed. Compensatory attention to the others can help but eventually the children's own evaluation of the bright child will emerge however much your own may have been suppressed. In the end openness, explanations and frankness are probably best. This is something they will all have to get used to and they usually will. Any kind of excellence causes similar problems. Good families overcome such problems with thought, love and care. Secrecy and deception are rarely right.

Underachievement

The bright child who is slow, inattentive, uninterested or mischievous at school is a real problem. The first need is diagnosis. Be sure the child really is bright before you intervene with the teacher.

Some bright children may have dyslexia. Only an expert can diagnose this and it is fair to say that there is much disagreement among experts about the subject. There may also be purely medical problems, such as hearing or sight defects which may limit comprehension, or some motor defects which may hinder writing and drawing. Have these checked and ruled out by your doctor. After that it is the social situation in the class that needs to be looked at. It is often a question of motivation. Has the child a reason to avoid success? Is the child trapped in the loser's complex, afraid to show its talent because excellence brings envy and unpopularity? Is there a personality clash between the child and the teacher or a classmate? Is there a hidden problem at home? A visit to a good educational psychologist may bring good advice. Sometimes a simple change of a teacher, or to another school works wonders and one never knows why.

Mentors

A mentor is a wise, experienced, counsellor and steadfast friend. The wordcomes from Mentor, the tutor who guided Telemachus in his youth. Mentor was supposed to be an embodiment of Athena, the Goddess of Wisdom. In the present context we use the word to designate an elder, experienced, successful, educated, family friend or relative who befriends, guides and helps a promising child. Most often the mentor is a parent who spots the promise of a child and devotes especial loving attention to its progress, guiding it into the love of learning. But there may be an aunt or uncle, a grandparent or a family friend who has more spare time or perhaps more education, knowledge and experience than the parents. Such a person may delight in aiding the development of a forward child. The literature is full of famous people, high achievers who pay tribute to someone in their childhood who took this role and to whom they attribute their success in life. The statistics bear out the importance of such mentoring. The Marland Report quotes research (see Chapter 1) which shows that highly intelligent children usually excel in later life but that only a small proportion reach what is judged to be their *full* potential. Investigating the common factors in that small proportion, about five per cent, it was found that in three quarters of the cases a figure corresponding to a mentor could be found in the background of the child.

The need is thought to be a general one by some experts. The break up of the extended family unit has created an unnoticed deprivation for many children at all levels of ability. The modern child often lacks the steady, loving, wisdom of older relatives that almost all children once had. With bright children especially, it is important because they need to be introduced to and learn to love learning or what I have called the World Culture, the stock of shared cultural treasures that has been accumulated by the educated from all cultures over many generations.

It is best, in the case of the bright child, that the mentor should be respectable, educated, positive towards learning, successful and experienced in the ways of the world. Mentors should be fond of children, patient and persistent. The relationship sometimes becomes a long term one. The child acquires a guide, philosopher and friend who is at hand to advise when needed right on into their career. The difference this makes to a career is often marked.

If a suitable mentor cannot be found in the parent's close and trusted circle it maybe that a teacher or other acquaintance will take a personal interest or find a suitable person who will. However, if this course is taken and the mentor is not well known to the parents the parent must be as cautious as they would be with a baby sitter or au pair, or any one else they trust with the custody of their child. They have to be sure that the person is above suspicion in the obvious ways. It is best in such cases not to leave the child and mentor alone until trust is fully established. The

Mensa Foundation For Gifted Children is cautiously experimenting with a scheme to help parents to find a suitable mentor for Mensa children if other means fail.

Telephone mentoring has been tried and works. American Mensa has Gifted Children's groups which sometimes arrange it. A bright child, even a baby, soon learns to call up its 'uncle' or 'auntie' when it feels like a chat or has a problem.

Homework

Often the only way of stretching a bright child is at home. It is very important that the very able child shall have a quiet, warm, comfortable place where it can work and study. There should be a routine, a regular time. The habit of regular work and study is of enormous importance. It cannot be acquired too early. It lasts for a lifetime. There is no greater gift you can give your child than helping it to find the solace and boon of joy in work.

It is strange that many parents will successfully insist on music or dancing lessons and find that they lead to a love of these arts in the child. Yet they rarely think of setting the habit of enquiry and study which can also be a delight throughout life.

If the school does not set homework you can find ways to do it yourself. If you cannot, then you may be able to find a mentor for your child.

Meeting other bright children

As I have said, it is important that the bright child should not get to be too sure of itself, should encounter challenge and competition, preferably from other children of its own age.

If you or your child is a member of Mensa (about 30,000 members in the British Isles) there is a chance of joining or starting and organising a Saturday Club for other bright children in your area. The National Association For Gifted Children (about 3,000 members) also has a number of centres around the country which organise such meetings.

Apart from this it might be possible to arrange such regular meetings via the local schools or even through the educational authority. Long experience shows that such meetings for mutual stimulation, friendships, joint study, lectures, videos, computer games, board games and just general fun can be very valuable indeed. There is not the faintest smidgen of evidence that this 'elitist creaming off' does the slightest harm. It does not *create* bigheads. It is the best *cure* for them, as the children find to their delight that there are others like themselves, with similar interests and similar problems.

Parents ought also to read Chapter 4, that addressed to the clever child itself.

Chapter 3

The education of the intelligent, a parent's guide

TO BEGIN AT the beginning I must ask a silly question. Does your bright child have to go to school? The answer is 'No'. Your legal obligation under the 1944 Act is this. You 'must cause him (the child) to receive efficient full time education suitable to his age, ability or aptitude, either by regular attendance at school or otherwise'. Education is compulsory. Attendance at a school is not. If you register your child for a school you must inform the head before you can withdraw the child. Otherwise it is up to the LEA to discover what you are doing and ensure that you are meeting the above legal obligation.

This answer to the silly question is important to the small but growing class of parents who take on the job of educating the child themselves. Some feel that sending a child to the state school which is offered to them is a failure to meet their own legal obligation. This is especially so in the case of the parent of the very bright child. The experience of DIY parents generally is that about half the LEAs insist on receiving a full curriculum and time table from parents. About half do not bother. Of course under the 1988 Educational Reform Act a DIY parent must teach according to the National Curriculum. They will have to arrange for the periodic testing too.

Education Otherwise is an organisation of around 2,000 parents who have taken this option. Joseph O'Connor, a spokesman for them, is reported as saying that his daughter who started school with an eight year reading age was given starter books with a few words on each page and was bored and humbled by the experience. He withdrew her and took on the job himself. He is expecting her to take GCSE in English and mathematics at 12 or 13 instead of at 16 as would have happened at the school. She will then have three or four extra years to concentrate on other subjects. The address of Education Otherwise is 25 Common Lane, Hemingford Abbots, Cambridge PE18 9AN.

Various cautious educational experts claim that a child who does not attend school might lose something important even if their education is satisfactory. Bearing in mind what a relatively new institution a state school is I beg leave to doubt that. Mankind survived quite well for thousands of years before there were any schools. A loving, teaching family is the oldest human style. But DIY parents should see that the children's needs for social experience and contacts are met.

Schooling for the intelligent child

Most parents will not be able to take up the DIY option for the education of their bright child and they need advice about their special problem in today's schools.

Parents gradually get to understand their children's educational needs as they develop. Their ideas and hopes, their interest or lack of it will probably be the most important influence on their children's educational progress. This is a guide to the education of the most educable children in schools.

First we have to accept that no general centrally organised system of mass provision is likely to deal with the extremes successfully. The most educable children are rare and all state systems cope well for the average but not for the outstanding or the exceptional. The MFGC gets thousands of letters which show that parents of very promising children often find themselves paying for, or wishing they could afford to pay for, specialist teaching for their children. However, the parent should be sure that private education really is more suitable.

In some cases that may be the best course but before it is pursued parents should be informed about the existing system so that they can find their way round it.

The British educational system is in a state of flux at the moment. It is trying to reorganise itself after a period of widespread dissatisfaction and fundamental legislative change. The parent will encounter many trends and influences which may appear to be contradictory as the system tries to adjust.

The maintained schools

The state educational system is the one that most children go to. It is administered by the Department of Education and Science via Local Education Authorities (LEAs). These are set up by local authorities. England, Scotland and Northern Ireland each have substantially different systems which need to be explored separately.

Grant-maintained schools

Other schools, such as Christian and Jewish schools, are partially supported by the grants from the government but controlled by a religious board. Apart from this we are beginning to have more and more schools in the grant-maintained sector where the school has 'opted out', after a parents' referendum, and are managed by a board of governors under more direct supervision by the DES.

The stages and ages

It will often happen that parents of promising children will be thinking of making changes, shifting children to other schools or classes to get them a more suitable education. These are the usual arrangements with which parents have to try to fit.

In the British State system, the maintained sector, entry to primary school is at rising 5 years, junior school entry is around 8 years, secondary school is at 11 or 12. After GCSE examination, sixth form college or classes start at 16, when other students usually leave. Sixth form work is that which is seen as preparation for further full time education at a polytechnic or university.

In the independent system (private education) there are normally different ages of transition for boys and girls. Girls start primary school at 5 or 7, boys at 7 or 8, both usually by examination. Senior school entry (again by examination) is 11 to 12 for girls and 13 to 14 for boys. Boys are expected to take the Common Entrance examination.

Sixth form work starts after GCSE examination at 16. The GCSE takes two years, so changes should either be timed to be before 14 or at 16.

If any change is to be made from the one sector to another it is important to look at the child's progress along the curriculum at the school it leaves and at the position it will be in the school it joins. Some intermediate cramming may be needed if deficits are to be made up. The National Curriculum, or NC, as it is gradually taken up will make this much more easy to do as there will be one accepted standard.

One of the most serious mismatches of this type you will meet is on language teaching. The primary level of the National Curriculum makes no provision for foreign language teaching, which is a pity as language learning cannot be started too early.

Another problem is that the usual education at the state secondary school does not lead towards the Common Entrance examination which is what admits children to the independent school secondary stage. It is to be hoped that with the NC there will be general adjustments which will make this sort of transfer less troublesome. Some coaching for the Common Entrance examination is likely to be needed when transfers from the state sector are planned.

Getting help from the school

Almost all modern teachers welcome the parent who takes an interest, who attends parents' meetings and encourages their child. Such parents are a minority in some schools. But there are still a lot of teachers who resent what they see as 'interference' from parents. This is the real problem area for the parent of the promising child in a system not geared up for them. As we ride out the dying educational ideas which arose in the silly '60s, the passing days of producer capture, we find there are still a lot of teachers and even heads who are sure that 'teacher knows best' and that parents, and especially those who are designated as 'pushy parents', are an obstruction to the process of educating children. Educational psychologists who are at the sharp end of these problems report that about half of the teachers or heads who are told about an unsuspected clever child react negatively. On the other hand there are a lot of teachers and heads who are pleased to be told, feel no reproach and who go to great trouble to help. The MFGC has had many quick, imaginative responses to the first approach.

However, the parent is wise to proceed with superhuman tact until the attitude of the school is known. Even with the best school a lot of tact is needed when a parent needs to say what amounts to, 'You could do better for my child'.

Pushy parents

There really is such a thing as a 'pushy parent' but not all those so classified deserve the name. A pushy parent is one who is using the child as the instrument of his or her own personal needs or frustrated ambitions. Often such parents exaggerate the promise and or the willingness of the child. An intelligence test is a good way to bring realism.

The parent should be sure that it is the school that they push, not the child. If they think the child is promising they should seek confirmation by getting a test done. Unless the child is pushing against and complaining about its limits itself it may be wrong to risk the real hostility at school that can be encountered if an approach is unwelcome. Such hostility is very improper but it happens and there is no easy solution to it other than the trauma of a transfer to another school.

Having said all that, it remains true that children hide their ability from teachers and 50 per cent of high flyers are not spotted at school. Parental concern about this is right, proper and natural. Conscientious parents must do something if they find that the child is being denied its legal right to suitable education. That is the position. The Educational Reform Act (ERA) is unequivocal. The new phrase is stronger than that in the earlier act: 'Each pupil shall have its particular needs catered for.'

The parent must do something, but knowing what to do is more difficult. Certainly a friendly, tactful approach is essential. Start from an intelligence assessment. If this can be an individual intelligence and educational test by a qualified educational psychologist that is the hardest to ignore, especially if it reveals that educational progress is behind expectations based on IQ. Apart from this it is best to take the posture of seeking guidance, offering another point of view for examination. Ask what can be done at home, how you can help. You will have to be politely persistent. Give the impression that you cannot simply be talked out of your concern but do it with charm and tact.

If you do not make an impression on the teacher things get much harder because you will have to be going over his or her head at the next stage. It is worth a lot of time and persistence at this stage therefore. The next stage, an approach to the head teacher, entails some risk to the present relationship between child and teacher. There should be hesitation. If at any stage your persistence results in real hostility there is almost no way you can win short of removing the child from the school. You will have tested the system to destruction. So as you proceed from the teacher to the head, and possibly to the next stage of the school governors, you should do your utmost to proceed with the goodwill of those who are thus bypassed. You might go with the teacher to the head. 'The teacher is doing her best but she cannot meet my child's needs with all the other problems she has.' If the hostility encountered is implacable, it is time to give up. Find another school for the child. The parents who pursue a sort of vendetta over a child with an education authority or MP do so very often at the expense of the child whose life may be made a misery. It is, of course, quite OK to pursue such a matter once the child has made a successful transfer.

LEA programmes for gifted children

At this time there are only 24 Local Educational Authorities (LEAs) which have active schemes for gifted children. Not all of them are effective. Exemplary is Essex which has an excellent one. Ask the teacher or head to contact the 'gifted children' official in the LEA if there is one.

'Statements' about children with special needs

Educational psychologists are those trained to give individual mental and educational tests. Where special education is called for under the Act, such as in the case of a retarded child, the trigger must be a 'statement' by such a one. But there is no mutually accepted standard for them. They are usually employed by the LEA rather than the parent. Some parents complain that they tend to reflect official views or that their reports are highly technical and hard to understand.

Other parents with clever, underachieving children consult an educational psychologist themselves and sometimes get a statement to the effect that the child is dyslexic (has a pathological difficulty with reading and or writing). This brings the child into the ambit of 'those with special needs' in the Act, and can be the basis of a call for special education.

We find some disagreement among educational psychologists as to who is qualified for the work and further disagreement also about the results of the tests. The whole business of 'statementing', as it is called, has proved to be a tortuous business for those unfortunate parents with retarded children. It can take years.

I expect that many more parents will want, themselves, to consult good educational psychologists for diagnostic purposes, rather than have the consultation arranged by a possibly hostile LEA. There seems to be room for a lot more work in this field. There are a great range of diagnostic tests and computer program tests which are used routinely in the USA for the diagnosis and solution of educational problems. There is little sign that they are used here and one wonders why this is. The purely ideological opposition to intelligence testing which has been evident for so many years has robbed the conscientious educationalist of a whole battery of useful tools with which they could improve performance.

The Mensa Foundation for Gifted Children can usually recommend a good, reliable educational psychologist for parents who need their services.

The Government Assisted Places Scheme

The government has introduced a scheme to help the high flyer pupil who cannot get suitable education in the state system. The Department of Education and Science can pay for partial scholarships for scholastic, very able children from families who cannot reasonably afford the full fees. Some of the good public schools and other fee-paying schools make places available at 11 and/or at 16 years of age according to the school. Interestingly and incredibly about a sixth of the places that are offered are never taken up so that there are plenty of vacancies (1989). The children of applicants have to pass an examination and they are then selected at an interview.

If your child is selected, a proportion of the fees, adjusted according to family income, will be paid for you. You fill in a form which gives your income and family circumstances. If, for instance, your income is below £7,000 a year the fees may be paid in full.

Unfortunately information on the Government Assisted Places Scheme is not available in all Local Educational Authority areas. Some authorities are still obsessed with the outdated down-levelling, egalitarian ideology and think it just and fair to deny bright children opportunities and the nation the benefit of their contribution, by suppressing the needed information. You should write to the DES if you are interested.

Higher education

If a young person has qualified for higher education it is fairly certain that the principle educational problems of the parent are over. It is now the student who should make decisions. It is beyond the scope of this book to help the parent or the student with the very difficult decisions at that stage. The student is no longer an exception with a special problem, he or she is just one more undergraduate.

There is only one point that I can add to what the student and parent will already have discovered by that stage. There is, in my opinion, an accepted view, a ranking of the status of the academic career that is questionable and is increasingly being questioned. There is still a view, especially among the most able students themselves and their parents, which values high academic qualifications and occupations more highly than other sorts of achievement. There is a creaming off of the most outstanding talent into the universities themselves. There is, of course, a very positive side to this. The succeeding generations of students are exposed to the very best minds. My simple question is this. Is the balance right? Do we not need more of the really top ranks of the able in other spheres of our national life. Is it right that so many of our very best talents are teaching and researching so that the vital industrial, governmental, financial and commercial decisions have to be made by lesser talents? Academe is the first to discover great talents so it gets the first choice. It can sell itself to the young people with little input from the competition. When the really outstanding scholar takes a masters degree or doctorate there is a decision point where judicious parental influence can be important. Let the other options be fully explored before a choice is made.

The high flyer at university

It is generally conceded abroad by many experts that British education at the top level is good, our best universities have very high reputations and still attract the many really high flyers from all over the world.

The child that can become a really high flyer is lucky to live in Britain in some ways. They have usually learned English as their mother tongue, the most useful language for those who can and want to join our present World Culture. There are openings in Oxford, Cambridge and a few other universities where the entry standards and the level of tuition in many subjects is as high as can be found.

That is the good news. Now for the bad news. The British universities expanded very rapidly since the '60s, partly to meet a surge of young people resulting from the Baby Boom after the war and partly because successive governments wanted to increase the number of graduates. There are not many outside of the professional educational elite who would not say that more has meant worse in this expansion. (There are too many *within* that charmed circle who would indeed complacently deny it.)

When universities expand rapidly, as British ones have done this century, it is inevitable that on the average their entry standards are lowered but this is unevenly so. Those which have the highest reputations, those which get the first choice of the best students may not lower them at all. Those at the bottom of the esteem ranking may have to lower them a lot. It is, of course, a self-perpetuating system and there is nothing that can or should be done about it. All attempts to equalise in these circumstances lead only to general deterioration.

I have heard otherwise sane, sensible and moral academics say that if you abolished Oxford and Cambridge you would vastly improve all the other universities. This is a thoroughly dangerous and grossly mistaken argument. Levelling, trying to raise the worst by abolishing the best is worse than a mistake, it is envy-driven wickedness. What promotes excellence in a free society is competitive emulation. What maintains excellence where choice is free, is reputation. A university is a centre of academic excellence or it is nothing. It is a coming together of good teachers of high repute and willing, eager scholars. Do not expect those who seek the best to accept anything less than the best they can get.

Reputation is essential, that is what attracts the talent both of lecturer and student. Public confidence will rank schools and universities whatever happens. The only way to stop that wholly beneficent process is to abolish freedom of choice. It is when bureaucrats, officials and authorities do the choosing that excellence slips away elsewhere.

The same argument applies to those very silly or very mischievous intellectuals and politicians who claim that if private schooling was forbidden, motivated, influential parents would see to it that all comprehensive schools became uniformly excellent. To believe that is to be excellent in gullibility or self-deception. It goes against all experience.

If you abolish that which excels you have done two things. You have promoted the second rank to be the new top rank. You have lowered the average standard and the best standard. If you now go down the ranks abolishing each new top level, you are reducing both top and average as you go. At every step you are doing nothing but harm. The outstanding lecturers and scholars you turn away from Oxbridge do not get rationed out equally around Redbrick, they slip away abroad or accumulate in another excellence centre which becomes the new, worse Oxbridge.

The set of people who sincerely seek equality of provision is a subset of the set which is receiving less than the median share of it. By definition this is less than half of any population, a minority. Given the fact of self-interest, it is very unlikely to be the most influential, capable and effective minority. I suggest it is best to work to the assumption that educational levelling, like most other sorts of levelling, where there is a freedom of choice, will get nowhere.

The message for every university entrant is, having chosen your subject, investigate the universities in order to discover their reputation in that subject.

The question that has to be answered somehow by every parent of a promising child is this. Assume that your bright boy or girl has come through our current changing, wavering, highly variable, educational system with flying colours, has achieved the right kind of GCSE passes and then stayed on for some years of sixth form teaching and obtained the required A level passes. Should the young person be encouraged to go on to a university or to a polytechnic, and if so which and when?

Frankly the answer is difficult. First the bad news. Universities are not what they were and they are constantly changing. As with primary and secondary schools the standards and effectiveness of universities vary enormously. Unavoidably, more has meant worse, especially at the bottom levels. Even within good universities different departments have differing standards and values. And with the shrinking of the world and the mingling of nations, there is a much wider choice available here and abroad than there was. To explore all the options is almost impossible. Yet choices have to be made. So look at some of the general factors that should be taken into account.

I did not go on from secondary school to university and neither did my friend Clive Sinclair. Each in his own way, we have had so far good, productive, fulfilled and effective lives. We have made our little mark in fields where an academic degree might have been thought essential. I am by no means sure that either of us would have been the better for it had we been through the university mill and been intellectually humbled when young and impressionable by its brilliant, mature, and highly articulate professors and lecturers. By the time I mixed in academic circles I was self-confident, widely read, self-taught, an adult with managerial experience in research, industry and commerce. My interaction with academe was very fruitful and led to innovations, inventions and ideas that might have been pooh-poohed away when I was younger. Most Mensans have academic qualifications but I have met a very large number without them and with a story like Clive's and mine. They have been no lower in the ranks of achievement than the graduates. So I am fairly sure that it is right both for the individual and for the system for a significant proportion of those who could have graduated to take different tracks.

Our social groups are the descendants of hunter tribesmen who were evolved for that lifestyle over millions of years. We have to remember the simple rules of a human group. The joiner, the recruit, has firmly to be put in his place as a neophyte. He has to learn the rules and discipline of the group and take his hierarchical place. The group structure and continuity would be threatened if he were not humbled at the start. The new undergraduate, like the recruit and the new boy apprentice, has to accept his necessarily low primary place in the group pecking order. That is probably a good way most of the time and for most social, that is to say group, purposes. But the occasional original, the creative innovator, the very intelligent one who starts a new paradigm, he or she might need to be a non-conformist, a maverick, an outsider because they are the usual sources of that rare kind of change – radical beneficial change.

My conclusion is that the university might not be the right place for *some* otherwise highly qualified students. At least not at the age of 18. They might be wise to take that path as adults, after joining other less dauntingly clever groups when immature, those where they held the higher intellectual hands.

So what if you are advising a bright original, a student with new and interesting ideas? Unless these qualities are accompanied by massive self-confidence it might be wise to suggest that university qualifications, if really needed, should be sought after the subject has made his way and found his feet in intellectually humbler circles. You might even suggest that he or she might do better to skip or delay the university phase. But this advice depends very much on the field of endeavour the subject has chosen. For some careers, most science research, medicine, primary and secondary teaching, those where entry qualifications are mandatory, there is usually only the orthodox path. Universities *do* accept the occasional unqualified lecturer.

Otherwise, for the student who is bright, original and creative or, as is so much more often the case, is not too clear what sort of direction he or she wants to take after sixth form work, it might be best to recommend a break, a year or two of industrial, commercial or other experience before he or she returns to education at a university or some form of further education. With falling rolls at secondary school, there is no shortage of university places these days and an intermission is much more easy to manage than it used to be. There are also various sandwich courses which are arranged, and often financed, by employers. (In a sandwich course the student is in paid employment interspersed with periods of full time university or polytechnic education.) The mediaeval system, the *Wanderjahr*, a year of wandering between apprenticeship and master status had much merit. That might be right for some school leavers. There is also the Open University.

After a few years, or indeed at any time later in life, the challenge of a university can be taken up by a more mature, self confident person with a much clearer idea of what they want and where they are going. They will be more critical and more demanding and a lot less suggestible. The student may have been able to save money to smooth the path of study. Britain is a comparatively good place for the outsider and the late starter. The upper echelons of many careers, even academe, are penetrable by exceptional but academically unqualified talent. Continental practice makes it more difficult to break through promotional and recognition barriers without the right certificates.

Choosing universities

What should our university candidate and his parents or advisors do in the light of the above?

Higher Education is thought of as a privilege for the lucky few. There is another way of looking at it. The candidate is choosing to defer satisfaction, status and reward for his efforts in order to qualify to make a more demanding contribution to the common weal in the future. He or she is expected to work and study hard, usually away from home, for several years at barely subsistence levels of provision in order to have a chance of passing a difficult examination and getting educationally certified at a higher level. Meanwhile the 'failures', the unselected, are getting a three- to six-year start in their career, more money, status, progress and seniority. The incentive for the 'successes', the undergraduates, to make these sacrifices, to accept this 'privilege', is that they will be qualified for more remunerative and/or higher status service later. The work they seek is more demanding, more difficult and more responsible. I am not saying it is a bad deal or that it should not be taken up, but I question the view that the chance to take it up is a lucky break or a privilege which should excite envy. Universities are not the only places where a bright adolescent can study if he or she has a mind to it. Going through that mill is often a help but many who have not gone through it have done extremely well and become well and truly educated. Professor Ronald Fletcher believes that the only real education at the top level is self education. Universities and polytechnics, he says, must be seen as no more than aids to this process. Once a bright child has become a really motivated scholar he will become educated in spite of, more than because of, some university courses. Mensa is full of well educated but unschooled experts and savants.

Obviously an offer from Oxford, Cambridge or equivalent top flight universities in Scotland or abroad, of a place to read a chosen subject ought not to be turned down except for very compelling reasons. The *cachet* attached to a degree from these universities is an important advantage, not lightly to be rejected. But otherwise the advice is: investigate, check on the reputation of the university and the department that offers. A visit and a tour of the university is worthwhile. The atmosphere and general standards can be shown up by the degree of discipline, order and tidiness observed. These are very variable and can be awful. A university in the tradition of the World Culture, ought to be an impartial, balanced, bastion of and forum for freedom of expression and opinion on all subjects. Political clubs and meetings are welcome and natural in them. But universities which are over-politicised or which have one-sided politics are not recommended. A sense of this can be gathered from the posters and notices that are posted around. Such places may simply be nothing but over ambitious but inefficient agents of 'irreversible changes in society' rather than places where education happens. Their educational usefulness is suspect.

Many professors and university educationalists with whom I speak are very doubtful of the value of modern university education in some subject areas. Some of the humanities as taught today are seen as soft options for less able or willing students. They command reducing esteem. Ronald Fletcher tells me that his own subject, sociology, as well as psychology, political science, and even philosophy are among these. Professors Antony

Flew and Stanislav Andreski, both Professors of Sociology, have written books which offer devastating criticism of the way sociology is taught at some universities. Too many lecturers in these fields seem to be teaching whatever is the latest fashion in the subject. The traditional plan, to give each student a rounded course, a tour around all the past fashions and modes of thought in the field is out of fashion. Art, literature, history and even geography teaching is variable and sometimes open to the same criticism. History and geography have been subject to some radical innovatory influences which appear to be ideological.

If the talents or ambitions of a promising student lie in these directions the student's parent or other advisor will have to be especially vigilant and exacting in making a choice or recommending one. One might like to get a look at the syllabus and examination questions. Three early fast-learning years of a very bright person's life is a big investment which should not be lightly made. To pick up a narrow, fashionable dogma which can only be useful to one who hopes to make a career passing it on to other students is a gamble, and worse, one with a low probability of a payoff.

Languages are a fair option for those with linguistic talent. The really expert linguist with several languages has a big career advantage in the modern world.

I conclude this chapter by drawing attention to a serious general problem which I first discovered from personal experience. It is the problem encountered by promising children from unpromising backgrounds.

On being too clever – a personal tale

Who wants to be 'clever clogs' or teacher's pet? I have a very lively memory of being the one horrible little, very clever boy in an elementary schoolclass in a very poor district. I could read and write before I was taught, I got all my sums right and was always first with the answer to every question. As a result I was hated and despised by all the other boys in my class. Being small for my age and defiant I was chased and cuffed, bullied and sometimes made to run a gauntlet of urine parabolas in the urinal. I excelled without hard work or study and got used to thinking of myself as the nasty clever one. I very much wanted to be liked by my schoolmates and later learned to use my nasty brains to curry favour with older, larger protectors. And I learned to hide my ability so as to be one of the boys. (Later I became a vicious little marbles capitalist, inventing games which enabled me to win almost all the marbles in the school.) When finally I did get to a secondary school of the grammar school type I was in for a great shock. I suddenly found myself competing with other bright boys who had gained by the extra stimulus of competition from their age-mates in a way which I had not. I had got used to effortless superiority and to solo study on my own track.

I never did get used to going along with the general curriculum and I had great difficulty in adjusting to normal class study. The usual options of scholastic progress had been closed to me and I could only continue with the solitary studies to which I had become accustomed. I became unevenly educated and it took me many years to correct that. I had become idle through insufficient challenge and worked only in my own way and at my own pace so that my examination results were erratic. The headmaster once told me that I was the only boy in the history of the school who had gone from bottom to top of the class one term and back to the bottom the next term.

The worst effect of my attendance at this elementary school was that I had been so derided and punished by my school mates for academic forwardness that I seem to have introjected the anti-excellence values of my mates and had acquired a will to lose. And lose I did. Much later in life I had an insight into this. I looked back and could see that I was building failure into the foundations of all my efforts. I noticed that it was always when my plans and schemes were going well that I began to feel nervous and apprehensive. This would lead to a relaxation of effort or turning to another track. The insight did not come until my late twenties and it was a partial cure. I was at that time a manual worker but my life changed completely and I have now had a successful career as an inventor, industrial technologist and finally as the managing director of a high technology company. And I have become a writer, this is my fourteenth published book.

I think it was worth telling the tale because it illustrates what I believe is a common syndrome. In my long period serving Mensa I have met many scores of Mensans who have confessed that they have a version of what I have called the Will To Lose or Failure Complex. They too attribute this to the negative peer group influences on clever children at school. One friend called it the Samson Syndrome. You build your temple up with great care and labour, and then you grasp the columns, tear them down and bring all down on your head. In every case that I remember it was the person educated in a school of low scholastic aims that confessed to this syndrome. One black lady from a poor district in Kentucky said that it was only when she joined Mensa that she found out that what was different about her was all right. She later became a university lecturer.

However 'fair' and 'just ' it sounds, there is a very negative side to scattering the really exceptional children, one here, one there, each in isolation throughout our vast educational system as is done under the principle of the age lock-step with the mixed ability class. If someone had given me an intelligence test in those days and 'creamed me off', given me earlier exposure to proper competition, things might have been much different with me. When, after my time at school, the eleven plus was introduced, that problem was solved, but only for a time. The reform was reversed and the problem has returned.

The lesson for the parents of a bright child is to watch for the loser's syndrome and try to counter it by explaining the very natural peer group envy. Get the child for at least some of the time into groupings where his exceptional forwardness is accepted and approved. We all learn by the pleasure-pain mechanism. Intelligence has to be reinforced and rewarded if it is to be developed and used. If the child acquires the loser's syndrome the intelligence is turned against itself and an unhappy self-frustrating person is the outcome. In some cases where the school atmosphere is unsuitable or hostile and the parents cannot overcome this at home, a mentor, mentioned above, an educated and intelligent uncle, grand-mother, or friend who can join with the child in an approving and encouraging personal relationship with it is a great advantage.

Chapter 4

A message for clever children

THIS CHAPTER IS for you if you are a very clever child, I hope you can read it. I have tried to write for children of all ages. So if you are older this may seem a bit childish. It will get harder to read as you go on but read on until it gets too hard.

If you are over four years old you should be able to read a bit by now. If you cannot then I have two things to say. Ask your mother or father to read this for you. That is the first thing. Then you should learn to read yourself as soon as you can. That is the second thing. There is nothing else I can tell you that is more important. Learn to read and keep reading.

Learning to read is a bit like being born into a new world. You cannot remember being born. Before you were born you were alive and warm and comfortable, tucked away inside your mother. You had eyes and ears and a nose and skin and a tongue. But you could not see. And you could not hear or feel very much. You could not smell or taste. This is because you were in a ball of water inside your mother.

When you were born, when you came out into the world, you opened your eyes. You could see but you could not make things out. Your skin and your ears were out in the air. You could feel and hear but you could not understand. You began to breathe. Suddenly, for the first time you could smell things as you breathed. All this, the light in your eyes, the noises you could now hear, the smells, breathing even, was all new. It was all a great shock and you began to cry. But you got over the shock and soon began to find out how to understand what you could see and hear and feel. You began to learn because you could see, hear, touch and smell. You began to learn because you could use your five senses. That was the first awakening of your mind to the world. You learned slowly at first but then faster and faster. Now you know a lot of things. But you still have an awful lot to learn.

Read, read, read

Learning to read is like being born again because once you can read you can learn much, much, more. Your brain has come out of the darkness again. It is the second awakening of your brain. It is free to learn all the

73

knowledge which is written down in millions of books. You can learn it all by yourself whenever you like. You do not have to wait for things to happen so as to learn from them. You can learn what you like and when you like. Seeing and hearing and tasting and smelling are ways of learning. They are like being carried or crawling, a good way to get around but a bit slow. Reading is like being the pilot of a fast jet plane. You can go further and faster and do it on your own. The most important thing about reading is that you yourself choose what you read, you are the pilot, you can go to a library and read whatever you like. You choose what interests you, what you can understand, what you need to read just then. Television and the cinema are good but you take what is offered. You do not decide. There is not much choice.

Getting on with the gang

If you are a very clever child you are very lucky in some ways. But you are unlucky in some ways as well. You will have some special problems. They will not be easy problems but you will be able to solve them if you really try. You have good brains but you will have to use your brains. Being clever is being good at learning things and thinking how to use what you have learned. It is very good to learn a lot. Knowing things helps you to find the best way to do the things you need to do or want to do. The more you know the better and more easily and more quickly you can do things. You can have a better kind of life if you are good at using what you know. You can do more difficult things. You can be more helpful to people you like or work with. People have to help each other because that is the way we human beings live. Everybody lives better when they all work together. The clever ones can find better ways of doing things. That helps everyone.

The older ones know more than the young ones because they have had a longer time to learn. Because they know more the older ones can help the young ones more. The children need help because they had not learned so much.

But some of the children learn quickly and learn well. They are fast learners, the clever ones. Other children learn more slowly. They can be nice, kind, good friends and great fun to play with but are not quick learners.

The clever ones learn fast and get a lot of knowledge and that is like being a bit older because older people know more too. So a clever, fast learning child ought to be like an older one and help slower learning children. They should do it the way they would help younger children. That is the human way. If you are clever it is like being older and more responsible. That is a bit difficult when you are smaller and younger. But it gets easier if you think about it and try hard. You will learn to help other children more. They cannot help you so much. Not until they grow older.

Getting on with older children

If you are very clever you have to try and understand this when you mix with other children. As they grow older children keep changing, they get bigger and stronger as they grow older. They get less childish in the way they behave, they get to know more and are able to do more things. Usually the oldest are the biggest, the strongest, know the most and can do most.

But clever children often learn very fast and can read and write and know a lot when they are quite small, not strong and are still a bit childish. The older children are puzzled by this. It is not nice for them when young children can do things they cannot do yet. They do not like it when younger ones know things that they do not know. They are not used to it.

It might be best for you to have some lessons in a class where you are much younger than the others. That way you can get on with your lessons and not get bored going over and over the things you have already learned. If you *are* in a class where you are much younger than most it might be a good idea to make friends with an older child. An older friend will look after you and advise you how to be friendly with the others. But even if you cannot do that there are things you can do. Try to find a way to fit in with the group the way you do at home. Don't be annoying or pushy or noisy or cheeky. Don't show off. Try to be kind and helpful. You might know the answer to the teacher's question. But don't shout it out. Wait until you are asked. Ask the teacher to help if you find all this difficult or if the others do not like you. If teachers understand your problem they will be able to help you.

It may take a time but in the end you will find your place in the class. Children usually get used to each other in time.

Getting on with the teacher

You have to understand that you may be a problem to your teacher too. Do what you can to help the teacher to help you. Always be friendly and polite. Don't be afraid to ask questions but don't interrupt. Try as hard as you can to fit in with the class. If the work is too easy and boring, tell teacher. If you can get on further with the work, tell teacher. But speak to the teacher after class, not in front of the other children. Tell the teacher if the work seems too easy and boring. Ask the teacher if he or she thinks you are ready for more difficult work. Say you are sorry if this is a nuisance to the teacher.

Being different is all right

Babies all look very much like each other. But each one is different from all the others in lots of ways. They are slightly different in size and weight. The hair and eyes and skin are sometimes different colours. Every one has a different face and we can tell them apart. There are a thousand little differences right from the start and, as they get older, they become even more different from each other. It is good that human beings have these differences. It would not be very nice if we were all exactly the same. We would be like a lot of toys stamped from a mould. It would be boring. One of these differences between children is in cleverness. It is just one more way of being different. Some children seem to be quick learners. It shows from the start, when they are babies. They usually get cleverer as they grow older. (Others are taller from the start and grow taller as they grow older.) These are just different ways of being different. We all have to know and understand these differences. We can get on better with each other when we do. It is quite important for each child to understand his own differences. That way he or she can learn how to fit in with others. A very strong child has to know its own strength. Otherwise it might hurt other children. A very clever child needs to know that it is clever. It has to know that what is different about it is all right. Otherwise it will not be able to develop its brains properly. The child will be too easily satisfied with its progress. But because you know these things you do not have to go around boasting about them.

Cleverness is nothing to be proud of

You were probably born a fast learner, so it is nothing to be proud of. But it is certainly nothing to be ashamed of either. You did not *do* it but you cannot *help* it. You probably cannot help being secretly pleased and proud when you help other children; when you are quick to solve problems. But it is not very clever to show off. That way children and people soon dislike you. The *really* clever ones soon learn to be modest, polite and tactful. Doing things and learning things is easier for them. So they have no call to boast. That is the really clever way. Boasting and bragging about what you have got or what you can do is childish. Clever children soon get past being childish.

Children who are not so clever sometimes get cross with the clever ones. The clever ones seem to learn so fast and get everything right. The other children wish they could be like that. They try and when they cannot it makes them cross and envious. Clever children soon understand that. It is easy for them to understand how the others feel. The others feel as if the clever ones are the lucky favourites. In a way they are. So the clever ones have a problem. They have to learn how to stay friendly with the others even though they are the lucky clever ones. The clever ones learn quickly. So they learn never to boast. They learn never to try and make the others feel small. They try to be friendly and helpful. When that happens the others soon get used to the clever ones and begin to like them.

Don't pretend to be daft

What is different about you is all right. So what you should never do is pretend you do not know something when you really do. That is a silly game which holds you back and does not help anyone. You want to be accepted as you are. You will be in the end if you are friendly and modest. Some very clever children are not clever when they have this problem. Some children get cross because the clever ones always know the right answer at school. The clever ones hate it when this happens. So, even though they are clever, they pretend they are not. They hide their cleverness. They pretend they do not know the answer when they do. They just keep quiet. That is not sensible. It is bad for everyone.

People have to be liked for what they are and not for what they pretend to be. Be yourself, but be helpful and friendly. In the end you will find your place in the group. You are different from the others. But remember what I said. They are all different from each other in many ways. They have different coloured hair, different skin colours, different heights, different faces. But in the end all the children get used to these differences. They get to be friends. The others will get used to you and your cleverness in the end. So be true to your talent. Develop it as best you can. People are going to need it. The world needs to develop its best abilities. So those that have more than the usual share of brains have to work harder. You have to be more responsible. When you grow up you might find you cannot use your brains because you kept them hidden when you were a child. You will be very unhappy. I can tell you that for sure because I have met a lot of people like that in Mensa. In fact I was a bit like that myself for a long time. But being a bit clever, I learned better. I got to be a lot happier afterwards.

Get your mother or father to read what I say in this book about how good it is to have someone grown up who can help you with the special problems of being a clever child.

For older children

I assume you are clever. Let me explain what cleverness, intelligence, really is. The word has a lot of different meanings but the one we are talking about in this book is cognitive or intellectual intelligence, the ability to get knowledge and use it well. It is not just how much you know, it is how easily and how well you learn. It is also how well you understand and *use* what you know. If a child learns to run fast or jump high or dance or do acrobatics we sometimes say, 'How clever!'. But that is not the kind of cleverness I mean, intelligence or intellectual cleverness. That is skill, motor ability. When we see the wonderfully beautiful judgement and precision of a bird flying or an ape swinging so skilfully through the branches we are seeing skill, motor intelligence. The bird senses its position and the feel of the wind with its eyes and feathers and skin and its brain knows just what messages to send to its muscles to do the right thing. There is no cognitive thinking. It is a wonderfully adjusted system with senses talking to brain and brain talking to muscles. Children and people have that sort of intelligence too but it is a different thing from intellectual or cognitive intelligence. You can be unskilled, even a bit clumsy and still be very clever in a cognitive sense. Think of Professor Stephen Hawking, the mathematician and physicist who is paralysed. He has no motor skill at all but very great cognitive intelligence. He is a genius. So what is the difference? Cognitive thinking power, intelligence, what we discover when you do an intelligence test, this is a human speciality. Other animals show little sign of it. Some of the apes show some.

Social intelligence

Cognitive intelligence is very much a social thing. It is the sort of understanding that can pass from one brain to another. Every ape or bird has to learn for itself but people can pass knowledge and understanding to each other in speech and writing. Cognitive intelligence has to be encoded into some sort of symbolic system, spoken or written words, mathematic signs, graphic designs and diagrams. In all of these, one thing, a symbol represents another. The word 'bird' represents the thing, the feathery thing that flies. There is a social agreement about the connection between the symbol, the *word* 'bird' and the object, the bird itself. I have this connection in my mind and you have it in yours. So I can make your brain think about a bird when there is no bird around just by saying 'bird'. With symbolic communication, thinking and learning can spread from brain to brain. It is no longer confined to one brain at a time. Mankind can build brain networks so that a lot of brains can work together in one super system. That is what intelligence is about.

Superintelligent systems

Science is an example of such a super system. A very great number of scientists are all in constant communication, reading each other's papers and checking each other's work so that a sort of general, well tested, shared, common knowledge pool or database is available for everyone, everywhere. There are many such examples. The commercial and industrial communications systems; the educational system; the financial markets all over the world; all these are inter-linked and interacting. They are learning and growing and developing. They are a bit like a very big brain with all the people in the system in communication with each other at the same time like the nerves in a single brain are.

The World Culture

I talk of what I call the World Culture. This is the biggest inter-connected network of all which is richly interconnected. This is the great database of mankind as a whole, a sort of World Brain. It is the combination of all the other world knowledge and know-how networks. It includes all the interacting networks, those of art, music, literature, philosophy, trade, industry, technology, law, science; all those where there is a common store of knowledge, ways and practices which are generally accepted world wide. This is the World Culture. Anyone who can read one of the world languages can be part of it if they are intelligent enough and ready to work and study hard. Every very well-educated person around the world is a member of the World Culture whether they know it or not. Education is nothing more than the process of joining, tuning in to, this World Culture. The educated, wherever they are, share in the carefully selected treasures of knowledge, understanding, know-how, and comprehension that the clever and educated ones of past generations have chosen from the many different local cultures all over the world. They do not all agree, but they all share the same market of information and data. I said that you can have a share of this world treasure that past generations have stored up. The word 'share' is not right because knowledge and information does not work like any other treasure. With a treasure of money or jewels we have to divide when we share – the more you get the less I get. With the great and wonderful treasure of the World Culture we can all have as much as we like or can cope with. If I learn something, it does not stop you from learning it. We do not have to divide, everything is available for everybody. It is like a magic heap of jewels where the more you take the more there is still left to take.

Join the club

One of the best things about being clever is that you can find a place in this great world-wide communion of the intellect. The best advice I can give you is to join the biggest and most important club on Earth. The club that has no rules or subscriptions or organisation. Yet it is the club that gives you power and influence. Being a member helps you to make good things happen. If you are really intelligent it would be hard, once you know about it, not to join the World Culture club, to become educated. It would be stupid. Now very intelligent people are sometimes stupid. But being stupid is more difficult for them. Please do not be stupid. The world needs to find and use all the brains it can. It has many problems to solve. Educated intelligence seems to be good at solving problems. Join the club, there are no subscriptions in money, you pay in reading and study which can be a delight once you get the habit.

Set yourself high goals

One of the usual faults of intelligent children is that they find learning so easy that they are too easily satisfied with themselves. If you find it all easy at school, you can get into a lazy way and think you are doing wonders. Effortless perfection is a bore. If the work is too easy you ought, tactfully, to ask the teacher to give you something harder to learn. Otherwise you will be sitting there wasting your time.

You will be lucky if you got to a school where there are other really bright students. It is more fun and more interesting to have some competition and be kept on your toes. But if not you have to pace yourself, that is tough but it can get to be much more interesting too. It is easy to see whether you are being too easy on yourself. You just ask yourself this question. How often do I fail, get it wrong, screw up? If it is never or not often then you are not trying hard enough. You are not setting your targets high enough. You are in danger of getting bored and failing to realise your potential. Learning is a matter of trial and error. We learn from our errors. No errors, no learning. Set yourself hard, exciting targets and have the fun of struggling to meet them.

Take chances, have a go

If you are well in front and all goes easily, it is the time to take chances, try another approach, have a go. I believe the function of the most intelligent people is not so much to guide and rule other people as Plato thought, but to be creative, to offer new ideas and options to everyone. Especially while you are at school, learning, getting ready for the world of work, it is good to stick your neck out a bit, take chances and risk failure so that you shall learn the more. All the *really* successful, clever people I have known have been clever, careful, calculating, risk takers, arm chancers.

Ask silly questions

There are many great men who have made their name by asking silly questions. Well, questions that sound silly at first. If an apple falls from the tree on to your head you might be laughed at for asking the silly question, 'Why did that happen?'. But when Isaac Newton asked himself this silly question he was on the way to finding a hitherto unsuspected law of nature. Never be put off asking. Never worry about seeming silly or ignorant. Never mind if people laugh. If you do not understand, ask and keep on asking until you do understand. People who know a lot got that way by not being afraid to seem ignorant. Those that are scared to ask stay ignorant. If you ask silly questions you will have the last laugh. (But it is best to hide it.)

More about envy

No one who excels can avoid envy, it is the price of excellence. You have to get used to it and learn to cope with it. You have to learn to handle it because it can all too often be the enemy and destroyer of excellence. A very forward student who does everything with little effort is bound to cause envy and it is easy to understand that envy. The one thing that it must not do is put you off.

However, if you follow my advice about trying harder and taking more risks with higher targets you will fall on your face now and then. The envious titterers will have something to titter about and, funnily enough, will like you more. One way is where the clever one becomes a sort of mascot of the group, the one they feel a sort of joking pride in and tell tall tales about. I have the feeling that the absent-minded professor image is a clever trick by which the professor copes with the peer-group envy by taking the role of a sort of clown. That is OK as long as his work is taken seriously. It usually is.

To the bright underachiever

I believe that envy causes underachievement in clever children if they are unintelligent enough to let it. This is the picture of that sad and sorry figure, the intelligent underachiever. Do you recognise yourself? I hope not.

The clever underachiever is against the school, is good at talking but bad at writing. He or she is bored, restless, inattentive. The child seems self-sufficient but is impatient with less clever schoolmates. He or she seeks the company of older pupils and does not get on with the teacher. Does this general picture seem to apply to you? Yes? Then you see what you can do to adjust to the pressures that push you into being so silly. It is no use saying that it is all unfair. Life has no obligation to be fair. We have to cope with unfairness and not let it get us down. If we react negatively to unfairness it only makes matters worse, makes people more unfair. Do not co-operate with unfairness, learn how to beat it at its own game.

Man is a social animal and lives in co-operating groups and communities. What is the place of the intelligent people in these? Societies and communities confer rights on people and to do this they have to impose duties on them as well. We take and we give. If you are intelligent you will probably be able to give more than you take because you can learn to do difficult things and be good at them. This is what others will expect of you. It is what you ought to expect from yourself. Your service for the general good can be and should be performed better and more quickly. A successful industrialist, inventor, doctor, scientist or lawyer needs to be very intelligent. These jobs take a long time, are hard to learn and hard to do well. So it is best to get used to the idea that you will be a good contributor. You will have to learn for a longer time and do more difficult work. But you will sometimes (not always) be able to earn good rewards for your more difficult and more responsible work contribution.

General education and specialisation

As the world is now, and the way it is changing, means that the need for clever, well educated and trained people is growing greater. Less people seem to be needed for their skills and more for their brains as our World Culture and this civilisation goes on. This is because the clever engineers and inventors are designing machines which replace human skills. They can even replace the simpler sorts of intelligent thinking.

So there will be more work for suitably educated and trained bright people, they will probably have to work longer and harder. It is therefore very important to find as many of them as we can and for them to get the kind of education and training that fits the needs of the world in the future. That is a big problem for the clever, educable children, their parents and for everyone else because we do not know what particular numbers will be wanted in what jobs. These things can change very fast. So unless your ambitions are already fixed on a job where the demand is good and reliable, it seems like a good idea for the very bright child to get a good all-round general education, and not to specialise in one particular profession too early. That way you can watch out for a job or profession that you want to do and which is also in good demand as you reach the educational decision points. In my opinion the more intelligent you are the more important it is to get a broad and general education. It is at the central levels of great world data networks that the most talent will be needed. That calls for wide-band generalist education rather than for narrow, specialist subjects. It is only fair to say that course is the risky one. It is not so safe and secure, it is adventurous, but youth is the time for adventure and I believe the need will be great.

Having said all that, there is one thing to remember. There are some professions where early specialisation seems to be the only way to excel. Most really able mathematicians seem to have started very young. Some of the very bright children might want to become mathematicians, musicians, singers, dancers, actors, chess players or even athletes. All these mean early specialisation if you are to stand a chance. These are very competitive fields and many fail to make the top level but if children are really keen and ready to take the chance, there is nothing against it as long as they learn the basics too. It is good to have a few good brains in these fields where lots of practice while you are young is the most important thing.

You are very likely to want to go to university or some other form of higher education when you finish school. I have assumed that you will want to consult your parents about that so I have written about university from the point of view of the clever student in the previous chapter. If you are a young student and are thinking about whether to go on to higher education you ought to read it before you go on to the next part.

Beyond school

Some, by no means all, of those who are clever have the right personality for leadership. Brains alone are never enough. But if a child has both a leadership personality and brains too, then that is a good combination. There are a lot who have the right personality but never think of trying. Clever girls especially seem not to get the leadership jobs. But we cannot afford to waste good talent. They should be given more chances and they should give it a go themselves.

Certainly leadership is a great responsibility, a lot of hard work, and it is not always appreciated. But it is very rewarding and very exciting. To be a leader you need to be one of those whose motivation is internal. There are some children, especially intelligent ones who seem, very early, to become autonomous. They like to do things in their own way and time. They are 'inner directed'. Others prefer to fall in with the accepted routine or the plans of parents, teachers, gang leaders and so on. These are called 'other directed'. Neither is right or wrong, good or bad, both are needed. It would be bad if everyone were the same. You can make a guess at which you are. But if you are autonomous, inner directed, it is worth getting practice at leadership. It will often be a struggle to assert leadership in an existing group so it might be best to try first in a newly formed one, one which you choose yourself. The next part applies to all those who want to be influential, to have influence on what happens. It is even more applicable to those who feel they would be good at leadership.

When you have finished your education you are going to have to use it. It is good to bear that in mind while you are still getting it. I am going to tell you some of the things which I have found out about using your brains in your career. They are things which you will never learn at any school. Using your education and your brains to pursue an ambition, to carry out a plan or to earn a living is often not as easy as it sounds. It is best to get some practice in while you are still at school, polytechnic or university.

It is interesting and nice to know a lot. But the idea of getting knowledge is not just to fill your head up with facts. It is what you can do with your knowledge, what use you make of it that makes it worthwhile. So while you are learning how to study and acquire facts you should be dreaming, scheming and planning about how you can use the facts you will know, together with your thinking powers. You use these to make the things happen that you (or your family, group or company) want to happen. Making things happen is the name of the game, not knowing how to or having a head full of facts.

The easiest way to make things happen is to do it yourself. You can make a wooden table, write a poem, paint a picture or plan a trip. You can do these things all by yourself. Start by making such plans. Think them out carefully, using the knowledge you have been taught, or learned, or can find out, to make a good plan. It is easy to find out the way to do things at a library. Ask the librarian, they usually try to help students if they can. Then carry the plan out as best you can. When you see the result think about the plan you made and decide where it could have been better and whether the result was what you expected. That way you get to learn how to make plans and carry them out.

Then you need practice at another and more important but much more difficult way of making things happen, one which will be useful to you later. You need to learn how to use your knowledge and cleverness to help your group or gang, family or company to make things happen. That is much more difficult.

First there must be a plan, not just your own plan, but something that fits in with the group's ideas. Perhaps someone has suggested an idea which you want to take up. You have to think up a project or plan to carry out the idea that will convince the group. Then put the plan project to the group in an attractive way. It is often best to win them over one by one. Then you talk about it when the group is together. This means preparing yourself by finding out a lot before you say anything. You must expect opposition, arguments against the plan. It is not worth doing. It will cost too much. It will take too long. It will be too much trouble. It is not practical. You have to have the answers ready for all these objections. It is best not to be too ambitious at first, try out some simple plan. Do not worry at all if it does not go smoothly first time, second time or third time. Persistence is most important. Keep trying – you are learning an extremely difficult and very useful art. How to make things happen. How to get things done. That is the real point of education. It is about knowing so as to help doing, not just above being a clever know-all.

After a time you will find that you get better and better at helping a group to make things happen. You can try more adventurous plans and more difficult projects.

Clever people have lots of ideas and they all seem marvellous when you first think of them. Never forget that there are any number of ideas and that very few come to anything. The real problem is not thinking them up but choosing the best ones, working hard and being persistent so as to carry them out. Thomas Edison probably produced more important workable inventions than anyone else and he said this: 'Invention is one per cent inspiration and 99 per cent perspiration'. Choose carefully among ideas and get ready for the hard work and research to carry them out.

There is one piece of bad news about being intelligent that must be faced. The intelligent tend to be innovators. They think about things and see what they think are better ways to do things. Sometimes they are right. But innovators are usually wrong. All the errors of the faulty innovators are more than made up for by the few who were right and who overcame the resistances that all innovators meet (and should meet). Clever people who take high risks are gamblers and I think that is a proper function for them. But it is good for all the units of society in which they work that they should be there to stick their necks out because one good new idea may be worth the trouble of a thousand failures. I have noticed that all the outstandingly successful people I have met have been calculated risk takers. If you want to reach the top ranks in whatever field you choose and you want to get there by using your brains then it is wise to develop a sturdy tolerance for insecurity. It is from the ranks of the adventurous that the excellent emerge.

Every member of a group has to accept the group plan. They all have to think that they will get some satisfaction from the plan if it is successful. They all have to be appreciated for what they do and of course they all have to know when they have failed to do their part. There has to be someone in the group who says 'Terrific' or 'Try again'. It is usually best if that someone is very, very tactful. The person has to know how to motivate people to work and strive for the group purpose. It is a leadership role but the person who does it is not always the accepted leader. A leader must be a good motivator. A good motivator is fairly lavish with praise and not too quick to blame. The clever motivator rarely claims credit for himself and is very generous in giving credit out to others. In the end everyone notices who is making things happen. Good motivators are tactful and careful not to hurt feelings too much when they point out how things went wrong when someone slipped up.

The motivator is almost always the most influential one in the group, the one who really decides, even when he or she is not the visible leader. Of course the good motivator often becomes the leader after a time.

There are two things leaders have to do. They ensure group survival and seek group opportunities. The first and most important thing a leader does is to keep the group together. Most of the time a leader has to see that all the things happen that ensure that the group survives, prevent it breaking up. That means seeing that all its usual activities and actions continue.

The second thing the leader has to do is to watch for opportunities to improve the group, enlarge it, replicate it (set up another one like it), improve it, or better its prospects of survival, growth or replication.

Generally speaking the leader has group support in his or her main job, survival, and group opposition in his or her second job, seeking advantageous opportunities. Groups usually oppose innovations and it is best if they do. The American President Truman use to say, 'If it ain't broke don't fix it'. This is bad English but good sense. If a group is doing well any innovation is a risk. It might be the change which causes quarrels or does something else that would break the group up.

As a leader you must be prepared for, and not resent, the natural conservative instinct of your group. If a group went off in a new direction without question as soon as it was suggested it would not last long. Every innovation is an adventure and has to be carefully considered. Tact, patience and persistence are called for and the leader or the innovator must pass that hurdle. If the leader cannot organise consensus, general agreement, it might be best to give up. Having said that I must now add this. A group that *never* accepts *any* innovations very rarely survives because it is certain that eventually something will happen which can only be dealt with if the group changes its ways.

Napoleon Bonaparte was very good at one thing. Fighting battles. He won a lot of them because he was a good, clever planner. Battles are bad things but we can learn a lesson from him and the way he won them. He claimed that his success was due to the fact that while he was fighting each battle he was always planning the next one. You can learn from that because it is equally true of any group activity. Once you have set your latest plan in motion and the group members are occupied with carrying it out, the good leader has started planning the next stage. When everybody was talking about the victory and saying how well it went Napoleon was not listening, he was thinking of the next battle.

Chapter 5

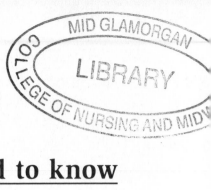

What teachers need to know

I HAVE CRITICISED some aspects of modern education in earlier chapters and this may not have gone down well with some teachers. Few professionals enjoy attacks on the methods and traditions for which they have been trained. But everything may be questioned from time to time. I know that many, maybe even most, teachers have doubts about some of the novel educational methods they have been taught or which have been imposed upon them by local authorities via (or in spite of) their heads. For instance, many Mensan teachers I talk to tend to confirm the view expressed by D. Naismith, the Director of Education for Wandsworth. He claims that a majority of teachers oppose mixed ability classes. They say they prevent them from doing their best for the full range of children in their care.

There may still be some teachers around who do not feel they need to know about the educational potential of the children they teach, who feel they can do their job without diagnosis, without making any judgment about the capacity of their pupils. However, I feel sure that there cannot be many who would still be indifferent if they began to suspect that they had an under-challenged, under-performing, really bright child in their class.

The majority of teachers, those who want to know, to be sure that they are fulfilling their responsibility to every child, will obviously want to use any available method of diagnosis, of spotting and challenging the underachieving child or of understanding the slow learner. When they suspect that they have an under-performing bright child, or if they want to know whether a slow learner is retarded or just lazy, they will be wise to use objective intelligence tests as a check on their professional judgment.

Unfortunately after the great campaign about the eleven plus, and all the anti-labelling nonsense, it became unfashionable for teachers to use any IQ tests. Modern teachers have had to rely on unaided judgment. Some, not nearly enough, authorities allow children to take what is called a 'verbal reasoning' or 'aptitude' test. These are euphemisms for what are really the so-called 'meaningless' intelligence tests. They are to be recommended and are often useful. They help a teacher to do what is so important: to check his or her judgment about the level of challenge and stimulus that is right for each child. The teacher, like the parent as suggested above, has to steer a course which gives the bright child, the average child and the slow learner the right ration of success and failure, enough to stimulate and not so much as to discourage. If the school does not provide the means I see no reason why the parents should not be encouraged to have the child tested. The Mensa Foundation For Gifted Children can help with individual or group tests. A letter to Mensa Freepost Wolverhampton will bring information. (Mention the children's age range.)

What is ideal is an individual test by an educational psychologist, but these are expensive since they take a lot of the time of an expert. Group tests of children should be conducted by a trained person. It is very important that they should be given in exactly the correct standardised way. However, the art is not all that difficult to learn and any teacher who reads the instructions carefully can get a reasonably useful first approximation estimate from a group test. The most serious risk is that of missing potential ability. I have quoted researches which suggest that group tests can miss too many bright students. But providing the test is correctly supervised and marked the risk of over-estimating the child's IQ is very much less than the risk of under-estimation. This means that very low scores or those below expectations should always be taken as provisional and checked against an individual test by a psychologist. Failing that, further trials in group tests from time to time are desirable. You can be fairly sure that a high scoring child really is intelligent, whether you have noticed it before or not.

The test given in Chapter 2 is based on a standardised but out-of-date published test. It may be used to get a very rough preliminary guesstimate of IQ. The publishers and I agree that it would be reasonable to permit teachers to photocopy up to 50 copies of the test per copy of the book for such a trial. The instructions must be followed strictly if the results are to be meaningful. It should be used as a first approximation guide, certainly not as a final assessment. If the results are extreme or very unexpected it is best to try to get a professionally supervised test as a check.

For a much more detailed layman's guide to testing I refer the teacher to my own *Guide To Intelligence and Personality Testing* (1988), Parthenon Publications. It contains two other children's tests.

Creaming off

The simplistic slogan 'creaming off', so often heard on the media, has probably done more harm to the education of British children than any other. I have argued elsewhere in this book that there is no adequate justification for the idea that an under-challenged, bored, envied, possibly disruptive, high flyer in a class is of any help to the slow and average children there. That child is not a volunteer, the State commands that it shall be educated, it is not sent to school as an unpaid conscript, as a help or stimulus for its classmates. It is there to spend its precious fast learning years equipping itself to contribute to the best of its ability and to become as well educated as possible, not for the sake of other children. Nor should children be shared out like sweets are, so that each teachers gets a 'fair share' of teachable children and dull ones.

Teaching promising pupils is very rewarding for many teachers and teaching slow learners is often thought less attractive but it is a more difficult job calling for more skill. The teachers are employed and paid to serve children. Children are not there to give satisfaction to teachers. I dare say there is more satisfaction in paediatrics than in geriatrics but we still like medical consultants to specialise and do not insist that the patients shall be dished out on a 'fair shares' basis, a ration of children and oldies to each consultant.

Getting the best from the slow child is a very honourable task and it is one that requires specialist skills, experience, and training. It ought to be well rewarded. But the job of getting the best from the best is also a specialist one which will be done the better for specialist training and experience.

Only a fool or an ideological zealot would think that these specialities are the same. It cannot be right for every teacher to cope with the full range when the differences are so great. There are few if any teachers who feel cheated when a child they have taught is 'creamed off' by being 'selected' for a university, yet many have been deceived by the 'creaming off' catch-phrase into keeping a very bright secondary level child from moving into a stream, track, class or school where it can be fully stretched, stimulated and taught by those who specialise in this kind of teaching. I appeal to such teachers to ask themselves whether it is the child or themselves that they are thinking of when they do this. There is nothing wrong with academic cream, the nation is going to need it. We cannot run a modern society on homogenised educational milk. Judging children so as to ensure the best for each is a vital part of the teaching task.

The 1944 Act puts upon the parent the duty of causing the child to receive a full time education, suitable to his age, *ability or aptitude.* The parent has entrusted that task to the school and the teacher. It is, I believe, the duty of the teacher to assess the general potential of the children they care for *in loco parentis.* They should think as a parent would, to identify those which can better be provided for elsewhere, or need supplementary provision. The teachers ought to do their very best to see that the children they serve are given those opportunities.

Teaching bright children

Forty years experience building Mensa into a worldwide organisation has taught me something. It has taught me that there is a definable class of highly teachable people and that the job of teaching them to the best advantage is a highly specialised and difficult art.

There are two sorts of teachers of bright children. Some, such as those who have had the bad luck to be teaching mixed ability classes, are not specialists at the task. The bright ones are just one more problem, not *apparently* a difficult one. Most *seem* to get on quite well and are no great trouble. The teacher will usually have to put much more attention into other children, the disruptive ones, the slow learners, and the average kids.

The other sort of teacher is rarer, it is the sort we find in the few schools, some private, some state schools, most in Northern Ireland, where streaming or selection is still the way. In these schools the teachers can specialise in the very different problems associated with getting the best from the really able child. It would be presumptuous and pointless for me to spend much time teaching these teachers. The teachers have usually learned their craft on the job and have become specialists. Such schools produce good results reliably.

However, perhaps I can be helpful to teachers faced by the serious problem of the occasional high flyer who is unavoidably conscripted into the age lock-step system, in the normal mixed ability class. I shall assume the teacher is responsible and fair-minded, has an exceptionally intelligent pupil which would clearly benefit from specialist teaching, has tried to arrange it and has failed to persuade the child, the parents, or the authorities. What else can he or she do?

Passing on the world culture

The best thing any teacher can do for a child is to communicate an enthusiasm for learning. Most teachers have long ago become infected by and attached to the great world-wide educational culture which is passing from generation to generation in an ever enriched form all over the world. Karl Popper calls it World III, H. G. Wells called it the World Brain. In my writings I have called it the World Culture. It is that consensus of choices, that selection, built up by generations of the educated and intelligent human beings from many rich contributions of the best from all past and existing cultures.

The Roman alphabet, the Arabic numeral system, Greek philosophy, European science, Indian and Egyptian astronomy; every continent, every past civilisation has added to the eclectic, accumulating treasure. It includes all the arts and sciences, literature, philosophy, mathematics. All the knowledge bases, as well as all the industrial, commercial and communications practice and know-how which have spread to many parts of the world because of the activity of teachers everywhere, they are all part of the treasure which educationalists help to preserve, improve and pass on.

The introduction of a child into this treasure house, getting it to understand how to use it, is just about the best thing that can be done for the child. This is so obvious that it is easy to take it for granted. It is by no means obvious to a child, however bright. The very first thing that has to be done is to find a way to have the child fall in love with learning. If a teacher can achieve that the rest will follow of its own. Educating the child will be a pleasure for pupil and teacher.

When school days are over, the work will go on until the child grows old and dies. If the teacher fails to convince the child of the value of education, the teacher has failed *tout court*. With the bright children this vital task is easier but is by no means to be taken for granted. We observe the fact that matched for intelligence, the children from educated parents (where these values are instilled at home), do very much better in education and career than those without that advantage. The bright child from an underprivileged home has only the teacher to rely on. Some teachers fall down on the task of helping a bright child to love learning. Some fall down because they fail to spot the high flyer child that hides its talent because of peer group envy.

Challenge without discouragement

Every child should have the right ration of success and failure, that which ensures maximum educational progress. The balance between too little challenge and too much of it is a delicate one and is different for every child, bright or not. The judgment must be yours and must be built on experience. If you do not venture over the border line from time to time you will never be sure that the stimulus and challenge is enough. Somehow you must set the bright child off on a lone venture along the path of the curriculum ahead of the rest.

First dismiss any idea that acceleration, advancing as far as possible along the curriculum, is or can be in any way harmful. Mensa has about 90,000 highly intelligent members all over the world and I have been meeting them for 45 years. Most of them have had accelerated education and I have yet to hear of any harm from it.

There is every possibility that you may get a child which can complete the National Curriculum four or five years ahead of its peer group. It will be very difficult to arrange in a single class but it would be unfair not to try. Once the child is literate it can be set tasks beyond the others and study by itself. To hold such a child into lock-step progress with the others is not education, but the reverse, it is the egalitarian policy of an educational Procrustes. The child would be better educating itself away from the school.

Separate study

If the class is one of those where the atmosphere is wrong for such serious separate study, it is helpful for some children if you find a quiet desk somewhere else, to set them defined tasks and leave them. It is not much but it might be the best you can do. Many Mensans report that is how they went through school.

It is probably best to give up any idea that you can be fair to, that is sufficiently stimulate, the very bright in any way that will not be visible to the others. The children will know, they cannot be deceived. Be frank with them. They have got used to the fact that some kids are taller, stronger, better at sport, than others. They have to live in a world where some are better at learning and they might as well know it. But targets must be set so that the bright child gets its fair share of praise and blame and is not seen as superior or a favourite in your eyes. 'I expect better from *you*', must be heard as well as 'Good!'.

Homework

I have said that some educational fashions are harmful. Those which suggest that learning can be nothing but fun and games are included. It is very important to all children and especially to the bright ones that they get into the habit of persistent work and study. A failure to acquire the work habit early in life is a serious handicap to any child. The Play Way, which involves merry teachers having jolly fun in disorderly classes of romping, playful children, is very hard work with very poor results. It especially wastes the potential of the teachable child. It is my belief that this applies equally to nursery schools.

Self-supervised work, homework tasks, should be imposed as soon as it will work for the particular child. It might be possible for the introduction of homework to be seen as a sort of advancement. 'Sheila has done very well and I think she is ready for homework.' Praising intelligence is wrong but to praise effort and responsibility is a teacher's job.

Enrichment

This is the slightly unfortunate name for the practice of giving forward, studious, promising children extra lessons such as those on an extra foreign language, or a musical instrument. Enrichment lessons might also be simply set so as to take the pupil further along, or go more deeply into, the curriculum which is already being studied. The vital point about enrichment is that it must be *qualitative* enrichment, not simply more of the same. There must be advance.

Enrichment courses are very usual in the USA where the numerous local branches of various gifted children's associations put pressure on local educational authorities to provide them. Many of these societies arrange them themselves on a voluntary basis. American Mensa has many local groups who do similar work. In the Soviet world the usual form is extra Saturday classes called Pioneer Classes to which it is an honour to be invited. The high flyers go to these.

Enrichment classes may take several forms. They can be arranged within the school itself and then they might have to involve mixed age groups. (I have argued elsewhere against the idea that there is something peculiar and harmful about the most normal human group there is, the mixed age group.)

Independent enrichment classes can also be arranged by the parents association, a local branch of a gifted children's association such as a Mensa Foundation For Gifted Children's group, or the National Association For Gifted Children. The local Mensa group can sometimes be helpful.

A local educational authority can sometimes be persuaded to set up special enrichment classes to cover a district. This idea was pioneered by Dr S A Bridges and described in his book *Gifted Children and The Brentwood Experiment* (Pitman). This has led to the excellent work which is going on in Essex under the leadership of Julian Whybra, the County Advisory Teacher For Gifted Education. Where parents agree, as many as possible of the really outstanding children in the district concerned are excused normal classes and go to one of the schools where there are specially selected and trained teachers and an enriched curriculum which caters for the special talents of the children. By this arrangement it is often possible to reduce the age range in the classes where that is found desirable.

Apart from the fact that they are able to advance freely at a much faster rate, the advantage of district enrichment is that the children are saved from the trap of effortless superiority. They learn that there are other children with their own level of ability and this is a needed corrective. They learn to strive and work harder and the majority of them enormously enjoy the challenge, competition and the interesting friendships they make.

The heads of the schools from which they come have to co-operate by making imaginative changes in the curriculum so as to be able to release the children without disturbing their scholastic progress. This turns out to be easier than it sounds because of the general advancement of this kind of child.

Another and obviously less satisfactory version of enrichment is provided by the summer schools for bright children which are run by various enthusiastic groups and organisations during the summer holidays in a number of countries around Europe. It is, of course, better for a very bright child to go to one of these and find itself among children of its own potential once a year than never at all, but a week or two cannot accomplish very much. The schools are of various types and most of them can be recommended. In my opinion those that pay more attention to serious study and opening new interests are much more use to the child and more enjoyable to them than those where the emphasis is too heavily on holiday fun. It is important that the sense of structure and order shall be well preserved. Children may seem to bask in 'freedom of expression' but experience shows that they fit into and enjoy a firmly ordered regime even more. The need for this must be explained. Details of these schools can be obtained from the MFGC at Mensa HQ by parents or teachers.

Enrichment can also, of course, be done at home. A teacher who is frustrated by his or her inability to challenge and meet the needs of a bright child can suggest and seek out what I have described as a mentor or tutor. There will often be a well-educated parent, relative, or friend of the family of the pupil, who can, given the idea and informed of the unfulfilled promise of the child, find time to lead, guide, tutor or help the child in regular sessions. As I mentioned earlier, the effect on each bright child of such an early influence seems to be very important.

Seventy four per cent of the small proportion who were judged to have fulfilled their promise had such a figure visible in the background according to the Marland Report. What such a mentor can do in effect is to 'sell' the world scale educational culture to the child. The child is given a love of learning which affects its whole career.

Acceleration, the non-problem

A wide reading of the literature and study of the practice of helping bright children shows that there are no really well researched and established solutions. The bright children are not only different from other children, they are very different from each other. Each is an individual, a separate problem. There are, however, many myths that have been copied from book to book unchecked and unproven. One such myth which seems to have no support is that which insists that it is right to hold back the progress of a bright child rather than let it be educated with other children whose progress is similar but whose ages are different.

It might be true, though I know of no convincing proof, that it is preferable if children of the same level of progress *and* of age can work together, but that is very difficult to achieve with the rare high flyers for obvious logistic reasons. If that cannot be done then acceleration is a lot better than no attempt at all to let the child advance as fast as it can and wants to.

This system of acceleration, called 'tracking', is quite normal in the USA, West Germany, France and many other places. It is one where the pupil works with the class which has reached about the same level of mastery of the curriculum as itself, regardless of age. There is no doubt of this. It is extremely successful. The only criticism I have heard of this practice is the unsupported assertion that it is `unnatural'. My assertion is that the extended family with the full range of ages from baby to granny is the most ancient and natural of all. If teachers cannot make it work we have to question their training and practice. The so called 'emotional problems' of 'differing stages of maturity' seem not to affect family groups.

How to signal success and failure

I often talk to school-children and I am sometimes appalled when I hear the way teaching is done these days. The fashion seems often to be this. The teacher takes great care to hide his or her judgments about the children. They are not given the results of examinations so that there shall be no 'labelling'. The teacher simulates a sense of indifference. Errors are corrected but with the sense that it does not matter too much. It is hard to see how this can help to develop a love of learning. When I ask children from these classes if they know which children are the 'clever ones' they immediately name names. The teachers have foregone the important incentive effect of using praise and blame, appearing to care, without even getting the doubtful results of seeing that there are no 'labelled' losers.

Now I was taught in a class in which we were all ranked in order from 'top of the class' to 'bottom of the class' and we were always shifting up and down the ranks. There were clear signals from the teacher who visibly cared how well we were doing. This incentive system was interesting and enjoyable at all levels. It was exactly the same sort of thing but with different rankings that was organised by the boys themselves, in the playground and on the sports field. It seemed to work very well. It was perfectly natural and harmless. No one seemed to see anything wrong with this system then and the school results were universal literacy and numeracy. The problem the teacher will have in the mixed ability group is difficult because the simple ranking system undoubtedly causes hopelessness and thus discouragement at one end and under-challenge, complacency and idleness at the other. The brilliant teachers who can do well in these circumstances exist but they are rare indeed. Their secret seems to be to carry the ranking, which my teacher did overtly, in their head covertly and award praise and blame on a sliding scale that takes account of the pupil's potential. It was not so much the rank as the promotions and demotions which worked with the old system. So the modern teacher has to make his expectations visible but attach value to those who exceed them rather than to the ranking itself.

Learning is a rack-renting business, the better the pupil does the more must be expected. That is what every child who has learned to crawl, then walk, then run, then jump has learned for itself. Enough judicious praise, not too much blame, raising the targets, these are the only emotional incentive tools the teacher has. Those who learn to use them skilfully deserve the life-long gratitude of those they teach. They often get it, all unknown. Bright children especially need to have their targets raised with great care. They are often very self critical, they raise their own targets too high. And they can be put off by an over-ambitious parent or teacher. But they can be turned into a misery to themselves and everyone else if, later in life, they find that the long years of education have been wasted. This happens when they fail to be infected with the love of learning and habit of regular work and study. They need this more than most children if they are not to feel wasted in later years.

As a man who has personal experience of these particular problems I feel I am in a position to say. I have seen the results of teaching failures with provably teachable people down the years. (Also, of course, I have seen the splendid results of great teaching successes.) I am sure of one thing. The happiness and social contribution of the successfully educated is much greater.

There are many reports by teachers who deal with very bright children that parental attitudes are sometimes negative. Parents can even feel threatened by precociousness, they find it 'unnatural' rather than simply exceptional. A bright eight year old can have the mental age of an average adult. Parents feel they are losing authority when they lose arguments with such a child. Nor are teachers immune from this. They are human and they are placed in a parental role, one in which they have to maintain precedence and ultimate control if they are to do their difficult job. A child who has learned the facts, but who has not yet learned adult levels of tact, can be an embarrassment when it constantly corrects a teacher or questions details.

Every teacher has to work out his or her own way of dealing with these problems because the best way is probably different for each case. But the essence is that the solution must avoid the most serious danger. This is what I have called the 'will to lose'. It is where the pupil enters a covert world which he or she does not share with anyone. The pupil simply hides ability, does not answer general questions, or do homework. It sets off on its own course in some obscure interest which attracts no attention and brings no success. The child finds a way of satisfying its urge to advance in the same mental realm without exciting the envy involved when it excels. It may get interested in some crank subject which is success proof. It may react with laziness or daydreaming. These are because it has been punished by peer group unpopularity for its previous overt excellences.

What the child must learn from these situations is that what is different about it is good, that it does not need to hide it. It has to learn its superior teachability may cause social problems with which it has to deal. If you grow very tall you have to learn to stoop in some doorways where others can walk through. If you are very strong you have to learn to be gentle. The teacher can have a private talk with the child from time to time in which he or she encourages progress and helps the child to cope with the problems thereof.

It is usually less embarrassing to praise the child that catches you out than to resort to some put-down or sarcasm. The pecking order rank of the one who praises is higher than that of the one who retaliates. But a private word with the child afterwards about tact and the need not to excite envy unnecessarily can be useful. The child needs to feel the teacher's restrained pride in its progress but not in its ability. An almost conspiratorial word after class now and again, 'Good, but can you do better?,' is the sort of thing.

Hidden ability: coasting, stinting

Summarising what emerges from the above there are three things to watch for if you have one or two bright children in your class. Hidden ability is the problem. The teacher may find it hard to believe what is reported in several researches mentioned earlier, that about half of the very brightest students are overlooked by teachers. The brighter they are the more likely to be missed they are. What I say above shows how this can be so. There are, I am assured by educational psychologists, still many teachers who sincerely believe that bright children are non-problem children and their duty is to worry about those with lower performance. The bright child who is getting by at a level lower than its potential is no worry to them. I do hope they will think again. But even if they do not they should be on the look out for the signs of what are called 'coasting' and 'stinting' which were pointed out by Dr Bridges in the book mentioned above. The child who is coasting is working well below capacity, just so as to 'keep up with the pack' and no more. 'Stinting' is setting themselves targets which may be above average, but being satisfied with a periodic 'stint' of progress which is below their capacity.

Watch for bullying

I have reported above that I was chased and bullied because of peer group envy when I was at school. I was a teacher's favourite but it never occurred to me to break the firm schoolboy tradition of never telling tales. A teacher ought to be sure that there is no covert bullying, in or out of school, of the clever ones who get all the answers right. This does not seem to happen in girls' schools so much.

Encourage autodidacts

The occasional really brilliant child is often a creative original for whom, once they are literate and numerate, self teaching is the best way. The evidence is purely from subjective impressions but I have questioned a very large number of extremely successful people. I have a distinct impression that more of them have been self-taught than otherwise. I remember one wise schoolmaster who asked for my neglected history homework. When I convinced him that I had been absorbed in reading astronomy instead he smiled and shrugged. We are dealing with the teacher who has the odd gifted child in an average class. If the child has developed a passion in some scholastic field which may be off the present curriculum it requires some thought before deciding whether the risk of encouraging such a distraction from work towards paper qualifications is important, or indeed whether there is such a risk. You can often bargain about it: 'Get your mathematics right and you can read your computer book.'

Do not discourage parents who teach

For the dedicated educationalist who sincerely wants to turn out more really educated people, the motivated and therefore often educated parent is the best ally. The minority of parents who are *really* interested have a visible effect on the motivation and studiousness of their children. No teacher can have failed to notice this. Parents can also be of great help in the teaching process itself if they know enough or are willing to learn enough. Yet there are some teachers who resent what they think of as 'parental interference' in their work. There ought always to be a way in which highly motivated parents can be integrated into the successful education of the child and it is the teacher who should try to find it.

Pushy parents

There are, of course, occasional parents whose ambitions for their children are excessive. There is a danger the child and or the teacher will be subjected to undue pressure. There are those who combine this with an exaggerated idea of the child's potential. Many educationalists feel that this can do damage and there are cases where this is so. However, there are many cases where this danger is exaggerated. We have so many cases where the parents who have been labelled as pushy have judged correctly and the teacher's judgment has been wrong when put to the test. There are still some teachers and schools where they push the problems of helping the promising child aside by claiming that IQ tests are 'meaningless'. Teachers and heads are on record as saying, almost with pride, that they have no gifted children at their school. One head mistress said to a concerned parent, 'What we want at this school are good *average* children'. She convinced herself that a probably very bright child was 'average', and withdrew extra classes with every appearance of thinking this was just and fair.

If there is a general fault in education today it is that the reaction against encouraging, and even demanding, effort from children which was practised without visible problems in my day has gone too far. There has been a general trend towards an undemanding attitude with low aspirations and a policy of levelling down rather than stretching up. The egalitarianism of the '60s emphasised that what is average and mediocre is 'normal', and of course it is. But if the teachers use 'normative' policies in this special case, if they take the norm as the *aim*, they can only reduce that norm. It is those above the norm that hold the norm up to wherever it is. Unless the high-flyers keep flying the average slips down. Since some schools have neglected them there is a widespread impression and some solid evidence that the norm *is* declining. Past examination methods have disguised this trend because they have been 'adjusted' so that the number of passes in each subject is kept constant. Under the National Curriculum plans this practice should cease.

One corrective for the 'pushy parent' whose natural love blinds them to a child's limitations is to settle the matter by having the child take an intelligence test. This is best done through an individual test by a qualified psychologist (which is expensive). A less expensive and reasonably reliable group test can be arranged by Mensa if nothing else is provided by the school. A first approximation guesstimate can be got by using the test in this book.

The other, opposite, problem must be watched also, the child from a very intelligent and well educated family that is underestimated by the parents because they have no idea what is average and expect too much. Again an objective IQ assessment is desirable.

Schools for gifted children

The trend *against* 'elitist' schools that 'cream off' cognitively very bright children is waning and there are a number of them being set up all around Britain at the moment mostly in the private sector. Many of these, however, provide scholarships or assisted places for very forward pupils. There is also, at the secondary levels, the Government Assisted Places Scheme by which children can get places in public schools or others outside the state system. Many of the places offered go unclaimed and one has to ask whether enough of the public sector teachers are seriously doing their job. They surely ought to be doing the best they can for the children who are compelled by law to spend years of their life under their care. The Mensa Foundation For Gifted Children tries to help parents and teachers to find places of this sort. Conscientious teachers who suspect that children in their care would benefit if transferred to such a school will obviously suggest the idea to the parents and try to help them if they agree.

Unacademic high flyers

If neither the teacher, the parent nor any other mentor has induced a love of learning in a bright child after a real try, it might very well be right to find some other target for the learning ability the child has been shown to have. It might be that the child is one of those where early specialisation is the right, and maybe the only, course. A vocational training or sport, games, or art might be tried to see if it fires the child's enthusiasm. Oxbridge is not all. The nation needs to find and train its excellent sportsmen, craftsmen, chess players, musicians, actors, artists, dancers, computer programmers. The top ranks in these fields may need to be both talented and intelligent. In all of them early specialisation and great concentration are known to be the road to the top. The Technical and Vocational Training Initiative (TVEI) has been set up to help teachers in this sort of case. They will send information to teachers who apply.

Chapter 6

Providing for bright scholars: the school management problem

THIS CHAPTER IS ADDRESSED to the authorities above the teacher in the school hierarchy. It is about the management of schools in which there will be occasional outstanding pupils with special educational needs and whose fully developed talents the nation needs. Aware of my presumption, I shall try to address the difficult problems and responsibilities that the national and local educational or independent school authorities have to face in this matter. The local education authority, the school governors, the heads of schools might find it useful to have a summary in one chapter of this narrow but none-the-less important problem.

The right of every child in Britain to be educated to the limit of its ability is, of course, unquestioned. The duty of the parent of every child, to see that it is educated in accordance with its age, ability and aptitude is commanded by law. When a parent registers a child for any school, the responsible authorities and the governors of that school have accepted the delegation of that duty. Every child is expected to invest at least ten thousand hours of its childhood in full-time education. Many children find that compulsory investment shows very poor results for them.

In view of the enormous variability of the educational results achieved with different children after the expenditure of about £15,000 per child by the taxpayers it is fair to expect critical questioning. After ten years of work and trouble by the teachers and ten thousand precious hours of effort by each child it is legitimate to ask difficult questions.

From the point of view of the nation as a whole and of the optimum contribution from every citizen can we ascribe exactly equal importance to the education of every child? A small proportion of children become highly educated, very capable and highly productive and responsible experts in various fields. The contribution to the national well-being and prosperity of this minority is incalculable but clearly enormous. Around 10 per cent (according to an ex-Minister in the DES) spend all those hours and fail to become functionally literate or numerate. Another large proportion seem to be little more educated at 16 than they were at 13.

Should the time, effort, and money spent on each be an equal division of the money the taxpayer has provided?

Where both parents and teachers have failed to motivate a child towards education, and the child spends year after year making no progress, should that child continue a hated and valueless routine long after it is obviously ineffective and possibly damaging?

No one can deny that there are such things as very teachable children. Most of them gain by and enjoy being taught and most turn into citizens who contribute well to the nation in their work later. The investment of time and effort in these children by schools, teachers, the taxpayer and by the children themselves is vital to an industrialised nation.

However, scores of teachers have assured me that they have gone through the motions of teaching many children for three years after the age of 13, knowing that nothing was being gained and quite a lot was being lost. This unfortunate minority of children were bored to death, hated school, often played truant, and wanted nothing but their freedom to start learning some occupation. They were often disruptive, a hindrance to the studious children and a misery to themselves. To what end do we keep them at it? This is a question to which I invite an answer. It will not be good enough simply to say that these numerous teachers were wrong or that they were not doing their job. Nor will it suffice to claim that the differences in educability are completely unpredictable.

Possibly these extreme educational failures could have gained enough to make those last miserable years of unwanted, conscript schooling worthwhile if they had been given different teaching in different classes, selective classes not mixed ability classes. Or it might have been better for them, for the school, for its staff, and for the nation, if they had been forgiven their forced draft and been honourably demobilised at some age below 16?

These extreme cases given above, the educational successes and educational failures are at either end of a continuum. There is a gradient between with every school leaver fitting somewhere. There seem to be too many laws and regulations instructing us here. There is too little informed human judgment.

Educational inequality

I have argued against mixed ability classes in a previous chapter. I pursue the matter from another angle here. As regards higher education it is generally accepted that inequality of provision is justified. The existence of publicly funded sixth form colleges, polytechnic schools and universities at which not all student citizens may gain a place reveals that, at senior levels, the judgment has been made. It has been decided that the education of some pupils is more important than that of others. What I have written above seems to me to justify that decision.

My next awkward question is this. Is it really true that no diagnostic predictions about educability will ever be able to be made before the child's secondary education is complete at the age of 16? Is it fair, just or wise, to command the presence at a specified institution, of a child for fully ten years when, as time goes on it becomes increasingly certain that the outcome, the improvement in the child's education from all that effort is going to be negligible or negative. The barely literate adolescent without a qualification is kept away from finding and learning a suitable vocation and forced to go on along an undesired, hopeless track. Is there nothing better that can be done? The anti-elitist, anti-selection fashion insists that all children along this continuum shall be taught the same stuff in the same class at the same time. Can we be quite confident that it is not doing a great deal of harm? Can the conscientious school governor or head be really sure that the all-in-together age lock-step class is the best for the children at two ends of the educability continuum? Can nothing better be done for the children who show great promise from babyhood? Some of these children can be as many as four years ahead of classmates. Can nothing better be done for the slow learning child, the persistently unmotivated child or the educationally handicapped child and the unwilling educational conscript. Do all these tragedies have to be played out to the last scene? I give no answer. I ask legitimate questions.

If the answer is that there may be better ways for the low achieving people for whom the school has nothing to offer at present, then maybe I have opened the door to the idea that there may be better ways for the child for whom the school can do a very great deal more than it is now doing. And by putting more effort into the willing and able it can do better at its basic job of turning out as many highly educated adults as it can within its constraints.

The problem outlined above comes from a very simple source. The simplistic idea that the innate potential of every child is exactly the same, or that no sufficiently reliable guide to it exists. The decision, in spite of the evidence of 80 years of practice, that IQ tests are 'meaningless' leads to the moral position that a teacher must never diagnose, never enquire about or think about the vividly obvious differences in educability that he or she observes. That one simplistic idea is what has done all the damage. The teacher tests this wrong notion to destruction on every single child.

It has been said, ad nauseam, that the IQ test is unfair to minorities from different cultural backgrounds. This in spite of the fact that some of these minority groups average higher scores than the majority on tests devised for other groups. It is true that tests are most reliable when they have been standardised on the language-cultural group they are to be used on. But it does not follow that they are useless otherwise. The objective standardised IQ test which has been statistically validated on large samples is fairer than any other means of judging educational potential. With the best will and training in the world a teacher's unaided judgment is going to be more variable, fallible and, yes, culturally biased one way or the other. The alternative of pretending to making no judgments at all would leave the teacher in the position of a juggler pretending to be blind.

The question that the school governor and head teachers have to ask themselves is this. Is it right to withhold any information, any diagnostic indicator from a teacher on the grounds that it is less than perfect. A doctor uses instruments to inform his judgment. Such instruments always have their limitations but it would be a poor doctor who failed to use them.

To encourage the teacher to know the teachability of his or her pupils is to save the children from being over-pressed or under-challenged, it is to discover hidden promise and fulfill it, to reveal hidden defect and help it. It is not difficult for a teacher to master the simple rules for the administration and making of a first approximation intelligence test. One teacher or two teachers in each school could easily do the job over a period. Computer administered tests are available which can do both the testing under standardised conditions and the marking.

Alternatives to mixed ability teaching

The better informed teacher ought to be offered various alternatives to mixed ability teaching.

'Streaming' is the old British system described above with A, B and C streams. Children are kept in age-classes but also classified for general scholastic ability so that at each age level there are two or three 'streams' according to the average educational performance of the child over all subjects. Since there is a high correlation between IQ and ability on *every* subject these streams tend to reflect IQ level. The clever children, the average children and the slower children tend to find themselves in separate streams.

'Setting' is the attempt, difficult to organise within the constraints of curriculum and time table, to group the children according to ability at each subject separately. The age lock-step is maintained but the individual child can be in the A set for English, the B set for History and the C set for mathematics according to its progress. Because bright children tend to be good at everything, it turns out that setting is not so very different from streaming. The children tend to be in the same set for most subjects. That makes setting easier to work than might be thought. It is, of course, possible to do a rather unsatisfactory form of setting with small groups within a mixed ability class. This seems to present impossible problems for a teacher. But it is better than mixed ability *desks or tables* I suppose.

'Tracking' is a successful American variant of setting but it abandons the most persistent and least justified British educational dogma; that it is fatal to mix children of different ages in the same class. Many countries advance pupils according to academic progress rather than age. Harmful results are not evident. The scheme is being tried out in Wandsworth under the direction of Donald Naismith, the Director of Education there.

This tracking system is a sort of educational 'market' where each child makes its own decision about how far and how fast it proceeds along the curricular track. It enables the child to 'pace' itself and match its capacity to learn to the general time table.

The time table is organised into ten week 'blocks' (units) of work or instruction so that they cover the whole curriculum in each subject. The child works its way through these blocks attending the appropriate class which is composed regardless of age but simply according to educational progress. As it proceeds the child attains a number of 'credits' which indicate its progress. These credits are used to guide the child's choice of class. It will join a class where the other pupils, of whatever age, have a similar number. This learning by stages rather than by ages is a well tried system which seems to be best for children of all levels of ability.

Donald Naismith notes that HM Inspectors' reports have said that standards in schools are too low because teachers' expectations are too low. In a mixed ability class, of course, they must be, they have to be adjusted to the slow learner and the average. Under tracking, he says, the children have a sense of 'owning' their learning which greatly increases their motivation. The system certainly has the great merit of increasing the child's autonomy during the learning process which itself is the most valuable lesson. The most important and the most advanced type of learning is individual study. Once the habit of solo study has been acquired education is assured, whatever the teaching. Class room study can be seen as the only practical way of giving most children the skills, desire for, and habit of individual study. Children are not passively taught, they actively learn. They need to be motivated. The sense of constant, measured progress during track learning must help.

There is a very small but important minority of children whose academic advancement and eagerness to learn is so great that, whatever the arrangements a school makes, they are hard to provide for. As I have said they are capable, if allowed, of being up to four years ahead of class-mates.

The obvious need here is to get the child into more advanced classes, preferably with other children of the same ability so that there can be challenge and stimulus between them. If this cannot be provided the more mature pupil of this sort, if he or she is capable of self direction, should be provided with a quiet corner where supervised but undisturbed study is possible. It ought to be possible to find a teacher in the school or elsewhere who can act as tutor, making occasional supervisory visits. Some of these high flyers show up clearly in class but others are only revealed by intelligence tests. The Marland Report disclosed that some of these 'secret superbrains' have disguised their talent so well that they have been classified as subnormal by some teachers. Where mixed ability teaching is to be continued, individual learning arrangements may be the best that can be done for quite a number of the more able and studious pupils, not just the really high flyer envisaged above. For the less mature high flying children of this type it might be possible to organise one teacher in the school who can take a single small class of mixed ages so as to allow the children to progress at their own pace. It seems to me that it might be possible to get parents or other qualified local people to come into the school to help with such special arrangements if staffing problems make it difficult. The so called 'pushy' parents of bright children are highly motivated and can be a resource.

Magnet classes or magnet schools

Whatever the reader in the education authority to whom this chapter is addressed may think about selective schooling as a general policy, I suggest that there are exceptional cases where it is appropriate.

Very few people see any great harm in selection when it is applied to very exceptional talent at ballet, drama, music, sport, horsemanship, athletics, acrobatics, chess or other games. We do not object when we find that very stringent and difficult tests are applied before some children are chosen at a very young age to go to such specialist schools. Such schools have often, over the years or centuries, built up a tradition of excellent teaching and training. Many are called to these schools but few are chosen. They are highly selective. Selection during schooling continues to be very severe so that many work hard to keep a place but fail to make the grade. We hear no stories about the harm done to the losers or the unchosen. We hear no complaints on behalf of those who fail to get a place or that those who lose one are being unfairly 'labelled' and ruined for life. And these selective schools for excellence produce a wonderful, living chain of talented performers whose work is a delight to all and a great addition to our national life and culture. And the losers shrug, walk away and find another career. This, according to egalitarian educational theory, can be done for any human excellence except the most important one, all round general ability, versatility, cognitive intelligence.

Many sincere educationalists find it easy to believe that the sort of high flyer schools for very exceptional cognitive talent that are usual in Eastern bloc countries and many others are unjust and dangerous innovations which cause great social harm. A few such schools do exist in Britain, in the private sector. They have created long standing, successful teaching traditions; they have accumulated know-how about their highly specialised job; they have learned what sort of teachers they need and how to find and train them. They too have a wonderful record at supplying the universities with first rate talent, as good as any in the world. The system has given the nation a long succession of world-famous scholars, scientists, writers and other savants. Examples of the great harm they do are hard to come by. Most of these schools offer scholarships, or assisted places under the government scheme. About 83 per cent are taken up, there are thousands of vacancies. There are, sadly, many LEAs which do not co-operate with the scheme for ideological reasons. They no doubt feel they are being high-principled, fair and just to the children whose chances they deny. I suggest that that idea is open to honest doubt. I feel they are failing the nation and their children.

Surely the public sector in education, if its supporters believe in it, should join this good and advantageous stimulus and competition? One magnet or high flyer school in – or even a number of scattered classes around – each area, should be provided. Here the really outstanding children can meet and compete in friendly stimulating rivalry. Selected and trained teachers can experiment with and perfect the highly special-ised methods which bring out the best from these unusual children.

If the need to mix children of all levels of educability for social reasons is thought to be vital, then let social engineering be divorced from teaching with which it has nothing to do. It ought to be possible to arrange such mixing for part of the time, in sport, at meals, at games, in play and in other ways, without sacrificing the optimum education of the nation's best talents.

Links with industry and commerce

One of the gravest faults in the British education system is perhaps due to its emergence from a long vanished aristocratic upper class tradition. Aristocratic education was preparation for the church, the political establishment and for the world of learning itself. Trade, industry, technol-ogy, vocational concerns, these were matters for the despised and envied middle classes. People in 'trade' were rather grubby and mercenary; one did not invite these parvenus to dinner. Now the intellectuals who systematised socialist views often came from aristocratic educational back-grounds and since the entrepreneur and the capitalist were cast as the class enemy, the aristocratic, non-vocational philosophy of education has been largely adopted by the left in politics. (The old traditional 'landed gentry' of the political right always adhered to it.) There was a consensus view that overrated the academic world as against the world of wealth creation and distribution, industry, commerce and finance.

However, things are changing and all over the country schools are forming better links with the world of wealth creation. We are beginning to follow the track of other more successful countries in this. From the point of view of the clever child this is all to the good. Of course, we need a share of the very good minds to go into public service and into research and future education, but the idea that these fields are higher and more important has been over-stressed in the past. The bright child needs, more than most, to be acquainted with the options in an open and unprejudiced way. There are arrangements called compacts by which students are ear-marked by companies. They take an interest in the student's progress and guarantee a job if agreed levels of achievement are reached. These are to be welcomed because it is right for some, certainly not all, children to choose a plainly mapped course early. Many of the world's great achievers have set their course early. But there is great need for generalists, all rounders, and they need to be very intelligent and very broadly educated.

Research

One of the things I have noted in this book is that many radical changes in teaching systems and methods have been made since the middle of the century without either adequate research or proper pilot trials. Compared with the enormous annual expenditure on education (about £1,500 a year on each of about 4 million children) there seems to have been incredibly little research as to the cost-benefit efficiency and outcome of this vast activity.

Like any sociological research, that on education is extremely difficult to carry out. There are few research teams in this field which start with proper impartiality. What research has been done seems always to confirm the prejudices of the research team concerned. The last study on the most important group of children from the educational point of view, the most educationally promising ones, was started in 1969 and never completed. No further work has been done since that time. The DES has funded a couple of projects recently but the experimental design and objectives are not very clear.

It seems that a serious study, preferably by a completely independent agency from outside the educational field, into the cost-benefit advantage of the whole process would be helpful in identifying the causes of the enormous variability in cost and outcome that is observed. Thus the more effective methods could be identified and promoted.

One proposal on these lines is to investigate retrospectively the educational history of a group of people who can be identified as educational successes and of another who are clearly educational failures. The outcome might be uncomfortably instructive if the research were properly designed.

The nation will have to face severe problems in education as the school intakes drop in the next few years. The graduates' age group, the 15 to 19 year olds, will have shrunk by one third by 1992. It will be more than ever important to identify and educate every student that can make the grade if we are to keep up the recruitment needs of industry and the professions. Research as to how this is best done is needed.

Chapter 7

Education as cultural heredity

THE PLAN OF THIS book has been to address a number of different audiences, the parent, the child, the teacher and so on. As I fear that not all of my readers will read all of my book I have permitted myself more repetition than I normally would have done. In this chapter particularly, I repeat and re-emphasise a number of things I have said in earlier chapters. I apologise to the reader who is reading the whole book; I thank that reader and beg pardon.

Bringing up bright children includes educating them. Indeed, since they are markedly more educable than many others they will absorb more education. In the developed world at least, and probably everywhere else, it is important to all of us that they get the chance and are persuaded to do so for the general benefit.

This will again be an exercise in reasserting the obvious, the forgotten obvious. The question, 'What is education?' has numerous contradictory answers and there is much dispute on the subject. A writer should be clear about what he means by education before he presumes to advise about the education of anyone, especially the high flyers. My book will be more use if I expose my particular positions and prejudices on the subject here.

Education has had many diverse forms over at least seven millennia since settled community life began. It might be hard to unravel the many motives in the many diverse societies which have educated children in schools. Recently education policy has been, even more than usually, under dispute. One widespread view, heard largely from within the teaching profession, is that its objectives are undefinable, not vocational.

This seems suspiciously like a soft option. 'Whatever it is that we educationalists do and achieve, that is education!' No troublesome judgments and quality control are required. No risk of cost-benefit assessment.

Another and more peculiar view is the outdated leftist one that the role of the cadre of educationalists is to change society, usually 'irreversibly'. Schools are there to prepare children for a radically and irreversibly changed lifestyle which they feel is on the way. How those who think so come to feel that they are qualified or authorised for such a taxing role is a mystery. Many of them are becoming a little discouraged nowadays because a lot of the 'irreversible changes' tried out in the Soviet world are being reversed amid general approval.

Compulsory state education

So we might be on easier ground if we ask a narrower question. Most education in the First and Second Worlds is compulsory for all children. It is usually organised by the state and paid for out of taxes, so we might ask what *state* education is or should be. There was nothing corresponding to universal state education before the industrialised nation state developed. That happened first here in Britain so we might seek a clue here.

Professor Ronald Fletcher in his book *Education And Society* (Pelican), suggests a simple and convincing definition which seems to apply to modern state education:

'Education is that dimension of society (and of all associated forms within it) which aims at the continuity and improvement of the social order; the preservation of approved values; and the provision of a basis for the fulfilment of the individual's life within the community with due regard to the individual's duty to the community.' This seems to be a fair philosophy for state education.

State education is much more distinctive, and less diverse, than previous educational systems. It arose and spread around the globe much more recently. It is so closely associated with industrialisation that it surely has a close causal connection with it. It seems to have arisen from the needs of industrialism and to have been an interactive cause of it.

Perhaps the traditional methods by which social units such as tribes, communities, cultures and institutions pass on the vital heredity of information, knowledge, skill, know-how about their lifestyle became inadequate when revolutions as radical as the agricultural and industrial revolutions of the last two centuries occurred. The Nation State began to assume its modern, more powerful and pervasive form in parallel with the development of communications and technology generally.

Preparing for a commercial-industrial life

It is 70 years since I was a child. At that time, what I write above would have seemed obvious. We went to school so as to be able to fit into a world in which the wealth creation and distribution systems were new and rapidly changing. We were still being shaken from a pre-industrial, rural-agricultural lifestyle into the new industrial one. But, after World War II there began to be a change in Britain and in some other parts of the Western World. USA, Northern Europe, and Scandinavia were first affected but France and even Germany and Italy also felt the effects soon after.

In these countries a strong egalitarian tradition had arisen in the 18th century especially among intellectuals. It began to spread to teachers and educationalists. These ideas had arisen from the British utilitarians, the French encyclopaedists and the American and French revolutions. A reaction from the previous, universal belief in the superiority of 'good breeding', of aristocratic *noblesse oblige* and royalty occurred and the idea that every human being was born equal, with equal rights and even equal potential became increasingly popular and influential. It had a great beneficial effect because it released an enormous pool of talent. Leaders, savants, experts, intellectuals and managers could now be drawn from all social classes and not just from those accepted until then as the natural rulers, the upper classes. The effect was an enormous leap forward of western civilisation. When excellence is promoted from a larger base population then standards rise.

However, the industrial revolution, like all revolutions, created many problems and disturbances to the settled communities which were affected. Most people benefited by raised living standards but there were many pockets and whole regions of new social problems. And, as standards rose, poverty and social conditions which had been acceptable became unacceptable when compared with the higher average standards. During these side-effect traumas and troubles of early industrialism, the principles of equality before the law and equality of opportunity were not thought to be enough. The doctrine of equality was extended and the principle began to be established (on the basis of repeated assertion) that people were really clone mates, all alike in potential and ability. The rich diversity of humanity was an illusion. All differences in ability, effectiveness, energy and motivation, and thus in an acquisitive animal, of wealth, are due to 'the system' and it must be rectified so as to abolish them.

On the other hand, as I have said above, the new science of anthropometrics seemed to show something that was not very surprising to earlier generations, that humanity was very diverse in many ways. Mankind diverges on many parameters of variability and that these differences were thought to have partially genetic causes. Attempts at measuring human *cognitive* ability showed, as discussed in Chapter 1, that there was no exception in this field, genetically and culturally, there seemed to be evidence for great variability in cognitive teachability – intelligence – as between children. So the work of Galton, Binet, Spearman, Cattell, Wechsler and others with intelligence tests, and the longitudinal work with able children and controls by the Professors Terman and Oden, came into conflict with the rapidly spreading and comforting faith in human uniformity. These differences seemed to be very manifest in the schools, colleges and universities that were proliferating and expanding everywhere. There were children who seemed almost unteachable and others who seemed to advance much more quickly than average and who then went on to excel in higher education and in their careers. All this was not acceptable to those who found the novel egalitarian beliefs so emotionally satisfying.

In Britain especially these invidious differences in mental ability spanned all social classes. They refused to go away as widespread affluence developed. So the intelligence test, the instrument which seemed predictively to reveal them, became unpopular with many among the majority of parents who found that their children were around the average or below it. The richer, more educated parents, whose children had been well educated at private schools regardless of ability under the previous system, objected to the fact that some of *their* children could no longer qualify for places at the schools for able, studious children because selection was now based on these more impartial tests of suitability. The exclusion from specialist schools of less academically suitable children of educated parents was, of course, balanced by the selection of a greater proportion of more suitable children from poorer families, but this group were often less politically articulate and effective. It was the educated middle class that knew how to pull political strings effectively.

So the dogma of human intellectual uniformity spread from the intellectuals to the middle classes and then more generally throughout society.

Minorities

The educational problems of the time were exacerbated by the influx to Britain of many people of diverse pre-industrial traditions and cultures. This was due to the vast movements and mixing of populations during and after the Second World War. (The many immigrants from industrialised societies presented no great problem.)

The new minorities from pre-industrial cultures were naturally expecting to be accepted on just and equal terms despite the educational difficulties arising from language and cultural differences. There was a sensible response to the new problems. Fears of social and racist divisions and conflict, such as there had been in USA, arose among the educated and intelligent. So in Britain the discussion or recognition of racial differences became taboo. As a sort of overkill, this led to the idea that recognising *any* human differences, including those of ability and capacity, was harmful. This was part of this rejection of what was thought might be seen as dangerous and divisive 'racism'.

The first egalitarian – Procrustes

At first this insistence on uniformity applied only to cognitive abilities and excellences. It remained respectable to recognise and salute excellence in sport or athletics. But extremist supporters of the egalitarian fashion can now be found who favour no-win sports and the elimination of any striving to excel even in these fields. These kindly simpletons were clearly fired by a genuine concern for Peace on Earth which they felt could only be achieved if we pretend that people are exact replicates, and that the natural, hunter-gatherer combination of co-operation and competitiveness which they cannot fail to see in every child is 'unnatural' and should be suppressed.

This well-intentioned political fashion spread widely and became very influential at the commanding heights of, and then progressively at all levels of, the teaching profession in some countries.

For many generations teachers had signalled success and praised and encouraged scholastic excellence. But many of the new generation of teachers were indoctrinated to see this as unfair. To recognise and encourage high performance in any child was to unfairly to 'label' all the rest as failures.

The new fashion was to keep up the pretence that the differences did not exist, or if they did they were due to unfair social advantages. Some even thought the teacher's duty was to see that inequalities of performance were 'corrected'. The word 'Procrustean', was used by Professor Flew to describe such teachers. (Reminder: Procrustes was the robber baron of Greek mythology who made travellers fit his bed by the use of the rack to stretch them or the axe to shorten them by amputation.)

So under this idea many teachers have been taught to try to reduce the differences in achievement between pupils. They put more attention and work into the slow learners and failed to encourage and stimulate the high flyers. Effectively they were levelling down instead of stretching up.

This policy started in the silly '60s, the days of 'flower power', hippies and revolting students and spread via teacher training colleges. The results are painfully apparent. There has been a long period of un-researched and un-piloted educational fads and fashions with a widespread impression of educational decline.

The sad thing is that it occurred in the United Kingdom at the very time when the nation needed to re-equip and re-design its industrial base after the distortions of a war. Britain needed to find, educate and train entrepreneurial, business, engineering, design, and craftsman talent. But at that very time, excellence of any kind was being discouraged (in many schools) by a child's first contacts beyond the home. France, Germany and Japan did much better than Britain here. After the war they all started massive programs of technical education which were extremely successful.

The 'British Disease' period in British education culminated in years of damaging teachers' strikes and a growing tide of dissatisfaction at all levels. The Government, the parents, the teachers, their unions, were all greatly dissatisfied, though for different reasons. There is a strong general feeling, backed up recently by the official school inspectors' reports, that educational standards have been falling and that the levels of literacy and numeracy have also declined. Teachers feel undervalued and that they have lost status. I can certainly affirm that teachers were better thought of in the '20s when I was at school than they are now.

Both here and in America there begins to be a vociferous call to return to the traditional styles of teaching. The over-emphasised egalitarianism seen in many schools has never become generally accepted by the public. The lower social esteem of which teachers complain may be caused by that dissonance.

Liberty, equality and fraternity

I think this trend has peaked however and today (1989) the urge to 'abolish' inequality is diminishing and the strange notion that scholastic excellence is somehow 'divisive' is being questioned. Things have begun to change and it is a good time to look back at the basic ideas upon which state education rests. Democracy is the chosen political base of modern Europe and this is coupled with the simple slogan ideas, liberty, equality and fraternity. How compatible are these? Fraternity is a *bond*. Bonds constrain, they must limit liberty. Equality of opportunity is incompatible with equality of outcome. People and groups diverge unless they are prevented by limits on liberty. So any society has to make some choices in trying to optimise outcome on these incompatibles.

Divergence by income, contribution, education, knowledge, and culture, will occur, are seen to occur, in any free society unless prevented. And such prevention constitutes a loss of freedom. At the limit it is naked repression. Liberty is *freedom* from bonds and constraints and to be free is to be free to differ. We can actually say that one measure of freedom is difference, inequality. This is not to say that the observation of inequality establishes that there is freedom. All free societies have inequality. Not all societies which have inequality are free. But equal societies, if any exist, cannot be free ones.

(It does not make much sense to speak of inequality at all, it is an idea almost empty of meaning because, looked at closely enough, every thing and person we observe is unique. The set of equal persons is an empty set. No one can point to an example of a society without an almost infinite array of inequalities.)

We must accept the extremely valuable and productive ideas of equality before the law, equality of opportunity in training and education, equal rights to respect and whatever social insurance benefits a given state can afford. We must accept the wonderfully potent and beneficial idea that no one should be prejudged on such an unsound basis such as ethnic, cultural or class origin. But none of that means that we may not judge at all. No society nor unit of a society can operate without making judgments and decisions about who can best do what. Human beings are evolved animals and hunter-gatherers, mammals at that. There are genetic, cultural and familial differences among us which affect our ability to fit into *any* particular lifestyle successfully. So some of us are more suited to this latest experimental Western industrial lifestyle than others. Those who do fit are probably less suited to other lifestyles. There are no absolutes here. These genetic and cultural differences cannot be quickly or easily changed. They are bound to create inequality of outcome unless we abolish freedom altogether. The Khmer Rouge showed that clearly when they executed 'intellectuals', identified by wearing spectacles.

The very process of evolution by which mankind came to be here on Earth involves two essentials, genetic variability and natural selection from that variability. Societal forms, cultures, human co-operatives and institutions must also be subject to evolutionary changes. Some kinds of society survive and spread and others collapse and disperse. To abolish trial and error experiments even in this field must be risky for the future of our species. Rich societies get so by tolerating freedom. Such societies raise standards of living for all citizens. They can afford to subsidise those who are unable to cope by reason of age, sickness, or any other reason. But if they insist on equality they are switching off the freedom which is essential to the incentive engine that drives the affluence system.

It is optimistic to think that our love of equality and fairness in this age is going to change the ancient aspect of all living things I describe above.

We cannot live so well without favoured elites. The professions are, for instance, cadres of experts without whom modern industrial society cannot function, they are elites, they are not a random selection. The professionals are *chosen*, passed through a strict selection process. And the choices are made on a necessary assumption of inequality of contribution and the requisite incentive, inequality of reward. This is true regardless of ideology everywhere in the world where the benefits of industrialisation have been achieved. It is probably true of every viable type of society in some degree.

In the Western world particularly, most countries are industrialist democracies and that calls for a diversity of systems of education and training and not standardised ones. This type of society depends on specialised skills, on many very diverse skills and abilities. As the range of goods and services in demand grows in these societies, so does the need for more diverse types of trained experts and specialists. And it grows exponentially. Increasingly the work of educationalists is that of directing pupils skilfully down this diverging tree of differentiation. Uniformity is exactly the reverse of the educational outcome required in tomorrow's world.

So should teachers really aim at equality of outcome as many still claim they should? We have no difficulty in agreeing that social actions, laws, customs and judgments should be applied equally and impartially. But they cannot result in equal responses and actions. It is absurd to think, as many seem to do, that the *outcome* of the judgment process must be the same in every instance. That is the negation of judgment.

If any educational process does produce equality of outcome we can be sure of two things. First that the able pupils who can contribute most to society have been deprived of the opportunity to do so and second that the average outcome is poor. It follows that we should judge education not by the uniformity of the outcome but by its diversity. Only when this is widest can we be sure that promising, able, motivated, hard-working pupil has been given equal, that is unrestricted, opportunity.

No society which fails to judge, condemn and discourage violent, feckless, disruptive, wasteful, polluting, criminal, stupid, unsocial, divisive behaviour can survive for long. Nor will a society succeed if it fails in the opposite way. If it fails to recognise, support, prefer, praise, and encourage excellence and social, altruistic, prudent, wise, productive and intelligent behaviour. This applies equally in the field of education as it does in the field of social behaviour and justice.

Further, no profession is free of the obligation to make judgments about the performance of its practitioners or of an adequate system for the quality control of its output of goods or services. Teachers are included among these professions, they too must seek and prefer excellence, judge, praise, blame and exert their influence to keep up and improve standards.

The teacher's part in role allocation

If we accept that preparing citizens to find a role in a modern industrial state is an important function of education, then it follows that the teachers of each generation should pay attention to the changes in the demands for various roles, skills, abilities and jobs. They should be aware of the skills required and the qualifications for these skills. For instance, the modern industrial state needs less muscular manual workers and more able, trainable expert technologists than before. Changes in educational practice should reflect that. There is little doubt that the kind of roles for which people are in greater demand today are those which call for difficult, demanding skills, rarer talents, those which require longer, more advanced training and education. The opposite is true. The need for simple, undemanding skills and abilities is reducing sharply. Unemployment is much greater among groups where, for instance, literacy and numeracy skills are lacking or below average.

Free countries try to provide equal rights and equal opportunities for all citizens but we are not born with equal willingness and ability to exploit opportunities. We are born unequal and into unequal environments. We can try to 'correct' natural scholastic inequalities seen in unwilling and/or backward pupils by limiting the opportunities of the willing and able if we think that is vital. But there is a heavy price for such senseless injustice. The result can only be a poor society with low standards for all and less security and protection for the poor, the old, the sick, the inadequate and the risk-takers who fail.

Even a glance at the GCSE results casts doubt on the extent to which educationalists and students are conscious of the importance of their choices in providing the nation with the next generation of suitably educated and trained contributors.

In a nation which is a great international centre of business and finance, and at a time when most wealth producers are at work in the business sector, we find that in 1988 out of 1,217,292 GCSE students just 28,957 took business studies (2.39%).

After a period under the influence of Procrustean egalitarians, teachers are beginning to return to the realisation that 'doing the *same* for every child' is completely incompatible with 'doing the *best* for every child'. The educationalist has to chose between equality of outcome and excellence of outcome. There is no way of levelling except levelling down. So if a sense of justice tells us to do the same for all we must be prepared to pay the price.

There is ample evidence around the world that humanity can be equal only in poverty, never equal in wealth.

The World Culture

There is one and only one truly multicultural society in the world. It is something that membership over many years of Mensa, a world wide community of around 90,000 comprehending people from numerous cultures reveals. It is what I have called the World Culture, the international culture of the comprehenders, the educated and intelligent everywhere. It is what educationalists are (or should be) procreating, protecting and extending. In those protean circles people mix with real mutual respect and with less than the usual amount of bigotry or hatred. As to the rest, we have to find the impartial imagination to see it all as a great moral Olympics in which all the cultures, all the moralities, all the lifestyles are in competition. We are entitled to back our fancy or the version of our fathers but, like it or lump it, the matter will be settled by the way things work out. I shall be able to tell you more in a thousand years.

As it happens, the way they are working out tends to justify what has been called Western Civilisation. I think it had an important and seminal influence in establishing the world culture. It has done well so far. But there are great uncertainties ahead. Can it cope with the enormously expanded population it has helped to trigger? It has lasted a few centuries, will it last millennia? Or will there be a catastrophe and a new growth from more primitive, tribal or religious patterns once again? All previous large empires and civilisations have fallen. But all have had successors. Thus far.

The implications for education in Britain of this view are obvious. It was fair and reasonable for the people of this land to start and follow the new industrial lifestyle which has brought unheard of affluence to about a third of humanity (but caused much over population and many ecological problems). It is reasonable for them to follow their star and continue that novel, risky, but rather wonderful adventure of the human spirit and the Life Urge. The education system would be moral, according to this new experimental morality, if it passes on to children the education and moral basis that can continue this line of development. If we have people among us who hail from other cultures and lifestyles we should honour and respect them and certainly allow them to live their own way. But we are entitled to defend our own lifestyle and do our best to pass on our own cultural heredity.

The incomers can reasonably be expected to be flexible enough to fit in with the lifestyle they have chosen to join. They can reasonably be criticised if, having made that choice, they insist on practices and behaviours that are incompatible with the hosts' way of doing things or which offend against their laws. If we had chosen, with their consent, to live within their cultural system we should accept a reverse obligation.

In a certain region of the world, a nation, an autonomous community has arisen and developed a way of preserving its traditions and lifestyle. It will certainly have to have an educational system which will achieve that end. It seems reasonable that those who find their own local lifestyle unsatisfactory and prefer to come and join the above culture would be wise and proper to accept its traditions, its languages and its educational system as they are. It is part of the offer.

If they try to reconstruct and perpetuate the lifestyle, the language and the educational system they themselves have rejected they may introduce into the host culture, if only as side-effects, the very faults and problems that drove them from the land of their own culture in the first place. In my no doubt prejudiced view, that which serves this developing educated World Culture is good and moral. It is probably less than 7,000 years old but I think it is the best thing that has happened on Planet Earth.

Making the best of the best

It is an elementary principle of good management, good organisation, successful defence and good government that strengths should be exploited and weaknesses remedied. It would not be a good government which tried to *equalise* its industries rather than to encourage, support, rely upon, develop and exploit the best. It might also try to help the strugglers in the middle ranks but it would be unwise to waste too many resources upon the worst except for compelling social reasons and briefly. The very basis of industrial success, like any other success, is specialisation, concentrating upon what you are good at. Just as creatures have to find and occupy an ecological niche so human beings and their institutions have to find, adapt to and exploit an industrial, agricultural or commercial niche.

With nations, with commercial companies, with any type of organisation, prosperity and stability are best achieved by those who can best evaluate their resources and best exploit them.

One of the most important but recently least regarded resources of the nation is the ability of the people themselves, the human resources, the resources of intelligence, knowledge, know-how and skill.

Industrialism had two contradictory effects when it was introduced. At first the spread of great mass production companies was achieved by the breaking down of traditional trades and skills into ever smaller and less demanding sub-skills. This greatly increased productivity by much reducing the complexity of tasks and making them suitable for a much wider range of workers. It also made work less demanding and more boring. A pre-industrial carriage builder started with square edged timber, bolts, glue, paint and so on. A small face-to-face team manufactured the complete coach. All was achieved with self-made tools using many skills which took many years to learn. Each was proud of his craft and of his skills. Work was a joy.

However, early mass production changed all that. A typical motor industry worker 20 years ago had a single repetitive task on a machine, at an assembly line, bench, spray booth or whatever. The work was so tiring and uninteresting that the whole industry everywhere became notorious for strikes.

Today many car workers are the supervisors, repairers and programmers of robots or computer-controlled machines. Once again the job is absorbing to the versatile, highly skilled trouble shooters who perform it. The demand for capable, careful, intelligent, well trained experienced and industrious managers, organisers, technologists, technicians, entrepreneurs, clerks and other workers has first waned and then grown strong again. The less demanding tasks are being taken over by machines and computers. This process may continue at an ever accelerating pace.

Time for a paradigm shift

There needs to be what in the philosophy of science is called a Kuhnian paradigm shift. T. S. Kuhn showed that science undergoes an occasional fundamental transformation when a whole current 'way of looking at things' becomes obsolescent and a new set of theories based on a new frame of reference is needed. It usually takes a whole academic generation because the change in the way of thinking required is so radical that the older generation are incapable of making it. The changes that had to happen in teaching biology and physics after the work of Darwin and Einstein were like that.

The changes of perception that we shall have to ask of British teachers if the nation is to have a chance of finding, motivating, teaching and training the best of the best for the next few generations is so great that I fear that many of the present generation of teachers will find it beyond their power. They will have to return to recognition of the simple fact that children are not clone mates with exactly the same genetic nature and possibilities. Like it or lump it, some through no fault or virtue in themselves, will be apt, quick and intelligent from an early age and others will be less so. And like it or not some will be dull, slow learners. They will have to recall that some parents have both genetic and cultural factors which favour the child's educability. Both the nature and nurture, the family habits and traditions are such as to favour the development of both intelligence and studiousness. These are the factors which lead to academic and industrial ability. They will have to accept these inequalities as a very long term problem and not their problem. Not what we pay them for. They will have to do the same as the rest of us and do the best they can with the material that is provided.

Their problem is to do their best for all the pupils instead of wasting time, talent and national opportunities in a vain attempt to pretend the differences away or 'correct' them by ironing them out or eliminate them by indoctrinating the children to change the system when they grow up.

The first and most essential task must be that of dealing with the problem of the children which have been called the 'high flyers', those children of really exceptional mental ability. However unfair we may persuade ourselves it is, it is upon these children that the future of the nation most crucially depends. We continue to neglect them at our peril. It is not a conceptually unified 'proletariat' which creates all wealth. One brilliant discovery by one exceptional young man or woman can bring a new industry and trigger wealth creation that will support many thousands in affluence.

Many of the golden ones, as Plato called them, these highly able children who can be educated and trained to do these things, go unrecognized in the present system. A number of researches arranged for the then Commissioner for Education in the USA showed that most teachers could spot the middle ranks of mental talent but often wrongly classified the very advanced child. There were many cases where the highly intelligent child was classified as subnormal!

Without the teacher's most important diagnostic tool, the quite wrongly discredited IQ test (the only reasonably fair way to pick out cognitive talent despite cultural and ethnic prejudice), there is very little chance that a very bright child in an often disorderly mixed ability class at a comprehensive school, in a poor district, will be noticed. Even if they are noticed by a perceptive teacher there is no provision for them. The rare, precious talent is left to lie fallow and be wasted, or worse, be attracted into entirely unproductive and anti-social directions. Their talent is wasted for the nation or perverted and misused. It happens. In many years in Mensa I have seen it.

The core curriculum and the periodic scholastic tests to be introduced according to the 1988 Act are much to be welcomed, but they will not necessarily reveal the real promise of the underachieving child which prefers peer group approval to high marks in examinations.

A special search for unrecognised high flyers should be started as an immediate project, and at all costs some provision, some special *selective* arrangements should be made to give such pupils the advanced education from which only they can really profit and from which the nation itself will *immensely* profit. This is what the MFGC is doing with encouraging success. As we go to press we hear that the D.E.S. is planning a fast-track scheme for promising children.

The sense of 'justice' which deliberately denies the children a chance to serve and equally denies the nation the benefit of their services is not only perverted but utterly crass. The best teaching is that which extends the range of differences, which most stretches all intellectual ranks and so does most to separate and distinguish the best of the best. That is the proper result of doing the best for all, it stretches every child and increases the span between the best and the worst at all tasks, athletic, musical, artistic and cognitive. Teachers who are bold enough to return to that excellent old code (the one under which the nation once led the world towards affluence) will find parents fighting to get places in their classes. They will also find that they will soon be making the nation rich enough to find the 'extra funding' and 'more resources' which they clamour for in vain today.

They will not be denied the salaries or the honour and respect that will then be due to the most important of the professions, the one which passes on the treasure of our nation and culture to new generations and has the honour and privilege of starting the great selection process by which the nation finds out that which is most important to it, the powers, the potentialities and the abilities of the next generation of its citizens. It is they who first oversee the ore and watch for the sparkle of a precious diamond. It is they who must first reveal those assets, upon the discovery and proper development of which, the nation's success, prosperity and continuity depends.

The future of education

I have suggested that industrialism became possible because state education was added to and partly replaced the mediaeval ways of passing on survival and living skills. In the 19th century, when the Great Switch to entirely novel industrial methods was going forward, there was no time for the old leisurely methods of family occupational traditions and apprenticeships under master craftsmen that were traditional. Kids had to know some science, be able to read, write and understand instruction manuals, and calculate.

However, nowadays the way we do things changes radically several times in a lifetime. The old apprenticeships tried to teach a 'job for life' technique or skill. So more than ever before, the future of the Earth's nations and cultures will depend upon the sort of education which the yearly 100 million new babies will get.

I believe in what Karl Popper calls the poverty of historicism. I think that prophesy about any complex living system is a very high risk undertaking. Any system which can learn by experience is subject to non-linear and fundamentally unpredictable changes. A widely publicised prediction can, of itself, either be the real cause of a radical historical change or conversely, the force that prevents what was predicted from coming to pass. (I think that George Orwell's *1984* and Aldous Huxley's *Brave New World* were books which tended to falsify the predictions in them.) The effective predictor has to be able to predict the predictions (and the predictions of predictions), their spread and effect. This leads to an infinite regression. And the poverty of historicism.

So in looking at possible futures for education I try to show some desirable changes and those which seem to accord with visible trends. I make no claim to prophesy.

I think we have to look at state education again and ask whether it is still appropriate in view of the enormity of the informational revolution which is in progress. The sheer informational *connectedness* of the world is vastly more than it was even 20 years ago. And it is becoming more connected at an increasing rate. State education is essentially a nationalistic phenomenon which arose and grew with the nation state. There are growing signs that the nation states are being drawn into much wider informational world scale networks and associations. To an increasing extent these networks are developing an autonomy. They are like markets, they have their own internal workings which are not in the control of any one human group or authority. The nations themselves are losing sovereignty as they join in larger blocks and networks.

Education and the nation state

One very important original function of state education, establishing national unity, has been widely abandoned. The weakening of the nation state has released a converse trend, that towards what might be called ethno-cultural separatism. The smaller cultural-ethnic units which combined to make the network of nation states are reasserting themselves in the First, Second and Third Worlds.

If we look around the world at the conflict areas today we see that they have almost all got this character. Russia, China, South Africa and many other African states, Britain, France, Canada, America, many South American states, India, Australia, New Zealand and many others; their principle conflicts arise from ethnic-cultural minority problems. And at heart such problems have an educational basis. There is a cultural clash which continues because different cultures are being taught to people in greater and greater contact. Each sect and division will go to any lengths to preserve its differences. Each demands that its lifestyle and culture shall be made to meld and fit in with the local national educational system.

On the other hand the truly educated and intelligent of all cultures and nations, because of the enormously developing mass communications system which has spread around the world, have begun to develop a sort of pluralist unity. There begins to be such a thing as world public opinion. The current subjects of and areas of debate, the terms of reference, the range of opinion options seems to arise from an unled world consensus. Examples of such world scale agenda setting areas of debate are communism and socialism, nuclear issues, pluralism, privatisation, space issues, biosphere issues. There are many other world scale issues where there is a world scale movement of opinion. The Gifted Children's movement is a very small example among many.

I have said above that it was the new enterprise-capitalist, nation state that probably spawned the state education system. The centralist nation states of the soviet world found it useful and copied it. We can now ask what educational changes will be required for the new world that arises from the trends identified.

Education tomorrow

Education tomorrow has to be more diverse, more pluralistic, less nationalist and probably conducted in smaller more diverse ethno-cultural units. The role of the nation state in education is probably set to decline. I see no reason to oppose the diversity of education styles which are based on religious or other cultural communities. Just as a rich, plural diversity of competitive wealth creation, firms and organisations leads to efficient and lavish provision of goods and services, so can a similar diversity of competing styles and methods do a satisfactory job of preparing and fitting random children into the world of adults. The one condition to make such a scheme work is the element of competition which is largely missing from state organised education today. The various ways of turning children into coping adults should be exposed to selection and rejection by parents, children, and employers (by the effect of various certification systems).

Given a plentiful diversity of systems and a competitive weeding out of the failures then the whole business of quality control could be delegated away from the worst places for it to be, with the teaching profession, the monopolistic producers of the service, on the one hand or the government on the other. The teachers are human and humans are self-serving. The government must always be much more sensitive to pressure groups like organised teachers or ideological politicians than to the multifarious, disunited consumers of the service who are not organised.

The passing of mass production

The present mass-produced, standardised education system is tuned to a passing phase of industrialism, that of the very large centralised mass-producing production unit. There are still many very large commercial organisations but looked at closely the winners can be seen to be very de-centralised. The successful ones are often little more than loosely organ-ised networks of largely autonomous profit centres. The big factory is giving way to the small semi-autonomous, cost-centre industrial unit. The big office is being dispersed and unitised. People can work to a big office or a tenuous international network from a keyboard monitor, fax and phone just anywhere. More than 60 per cent of workers in an advanced country like Britain handle nothing but information. Information, with modern communications, is ubiquitous, it has no locality, it is infinitely replicable. It is very expensive to move people and very cheap to move data. It makes more sense to take data to people than to take people to data. This is bound to affect the shape and style of education in the future. With educated mothers and fathers able to work from home; with numerous television channels, interactive video, fax, telephones, possible future sound-and-vision phones, a lot more of education will be able to happen at home and be supervised by a distant tutor or computer.

There are, of course, parts of the education process which require school attendance and they will continue, but the balance between school work and home work will drastically change. Schools will become smaller, more variable, more individualistic, more specialised so as to take care of the growing need for diversity of outcome. Instead of aiming for a relatively uniform product they will be seeking to satisfy market niches of greater and greater diversity. The broad distinctions within the system, primary, secondary, technical, sixth form, university, will melt away into a thousand different specialised forms.

The position and influence of the central government and even of the local authority will diminish gradually as the pressure of the day-to-day needs and requirements are expressed through ever more quickly acting and sensitive information networks. State education will wither on the vine as a million more lusty shoots thrust themselves up. But each religious and other type of sub-culture, fighting for its own survival, will no doubt call the children of its faithful in to schools where their local competitive sub-culture can be passed on.

It seems to me that nursery education, especially for the most educable children, will flourish in the future. But it will be very different from the present 'play-way' model. Eagerly learning, inquisitive and very teachable toddlers will get what they really want, real teaching from multilingual, well-educated specialists. The most precious early learning years will be used, not wasted, as they often are now, by child minding nannies who simply pacify and amuse.

The death of state schooling

What will be left of centralist education after the changes I expect? It will be largely what it started with before the industrial revolution. The great international centres of excellence, the universities and other important centres of research and scholarship will continue and develop. Though even these may be more dispersed than they are now.

There will be untold thousands of small units where special equipment and special skills will be brought together to serve carefully selected suitable pupils in learning and training for an enormous range of specialist occupational, artistic, musical, scientific and other arts and skills and roles. They will be under no one central control, no more than factories and shops are today. They will be under loose public supervision, as factories and shops are today. And the thousands of photocopied schools, teaching photocopied British Standard Pupils, classified by age, and learning photocopied lessons in photocopied unclassified classes will become a curious relic of an incomprehensible past.

But since I expect that the Solar System is the next frontier for the onward march of mankind, I would certainly expect there to be large and important centres where people, starting with children, will be brought up, educated and trained with a view to preparing them for an entirely new lifestyle, that in orbiting space stations. The adaption called for by which a creature, evolved to be a good hunter-gatherer, is turned into a modern citizen, was enormous but mankind achieved it, by and large. The adaption that will be called for as mankind takes the Life Urge off the planet Earth will be even greater. Education and training institutions and methods as yet undreamed of may be required. But they will emerge.

Chapter 8

British state education, recent problems

IN THIS CHAPTER I look at education in the UK and I am going to do so with my mind on the special problem of the very intelligent child.

British education is largely a national and local service and has been controlled by a succession of central and local party politicians as they replace one another in control at successive elections. But there is no continuing, generally accepted, underlying philosophy and therefore there is a wide range of incompatible views about the aims and methods of education.

There is no better system of government than democracy. But the trouble with democratic party politics is that politicians have to stand on simple, distinctive and contrasting electoral platforms. So they are tempted to polarise upon contentious issues and over-emphasise differences. State educational policy among others, tends to suffer from a succession of switches which reflect these polarisations. In other fields for example, whole industries have been nationalized, privatized and then nationalized again, then privatized yet again. This is not the most brilliant way to govern an industry or anything else.

So there is no clear long-term thread of national educational policy or standards against which the work of schools and colleges can be assessed.

In such situations what always happens is that those who are in detailed, day-to-day management of the activity develop an out-of-touch bureaucracy which tends to become less sensitive to the strategic levels at the centre, less responsive to government signals. An internal clerisy or *aparatchiki* arises which fights for the continuity which is the essence of any kind of organised activity. Now in a state-funded service the power of the consumer (and purchaser) of the service passes at infrequent elections to the government (national and local) and only down from that through numerous bureaucratic strata to the provider. So the need and desire signals from the paying consumers, parents, children and employers are very attenuated indeed, if effective at all. Some highly determined and vocal parents have a certain amount of 'nuisance value' influence, most have little or none. That, however, is the past, things are to change. The parental influence is to increase with the 1988 Act (ERA) and provided the parent governors assert themselves things should improve.

The system of education was supposed to be loosely centrally controlled and funded from rates and taxes, but the tactical, detailed control was with numerous local authorities. Originally these had been mostly controlled by councillors who were local, educated, middle class worthies and business people but with the rise of the working class movement, many local authorities became dominated by trade union and socialist politicians. The teachers' unions and those of other school workers were especially interested, so what happened could have been described as producer capture. The whole system became insensitive to the pressures from the consumers, the pupils and their parents, and over sensitive to signals from the educational trade unions, the teachers and local government servants. And the normal bureaucratic expansion was inevitable. By 1984 no less than 40 per cent of the 900,000 employees of the state education system were non-teaching administrators and supervisors of various kinds.

So we may understand more about modern British education if we look at the standards and values of the intermediate cadres and local layers of the educational organisation than if we look at the stated policies, Acts and regulations coming from Parliament. These cadres typically develop their own internal views, policies, philosophies and priorities. These can be utterly different from those of the general public or from the needs of the society concerned. The story below traces out the stages by which the present yawning gap between the attitudes and aims of the inward-facing clerisy of the education professionals and those of the ordinary educated citizen developed up till the days of the current reforms.

The four phases of 20th century British educational policy

Educational policy at the tactical level has come under several main ideological influences during this century and a way of understanding them is to see them as four main trends several of which partially overlap in time.

Phase 1: the universal education phase

I shall start with the first period I remember, the period when education was being extended to all children regardless of ability and sex.

Phyllis M. Pickard in her excellent book *If You Think Your Child Is Gifted* gives an excellent account of the history of British education. It appears that free education, at least for clever boys, had been available for many centuries in England. It arose from the need to recruit able clerics for the Church. This was the traditional system upon which Britain had risen to be the workshop of the world and the master of a world-wide empire. However, in 1881 after an explosive spread of privately and locally organised general education, compulsory universal education was introduced in Britain. Previously education had attracted much money from charity and this had been used to award scholarships, for bright boys only, to fee-paying schools. From 1881 onwards all children rich and poor, girls and boys, regardless of the ability of their parents to pay, were offered schooling. Both sexes and all ability levels were now to be taught. The previous schools had been largely adapted to fee-paying scholars and 'scholarship boys'; a selection of literate, clever, poor boys on the one hand and boys from middle and upper class families selected by an entrance examination on the other. Their genetic and social heredity made them more likely to be willing scholars. After 1891, with the sudden expansion of schools, as more children at lower levels of ability, motivation and coming from differing family tradition went to schools, the standards of teaching must necessarily have been lower than those which prevailed in the previous all- selective schools. With the enormous increase in school population the demand for teachers must have been very great indeed. Such a sudden demand for bright, educated men and women must have made it necessary to lower the standards of intelligence and scholarship that could be demanded from applicants.

So with universal education there was a new problem, the slower, less motivated learners who would not have been at school at all before. And an unavoidable lowering of the standards of the teacher intake. To be fair to them, teachers could do no other than reduce the pace of learning and the standards of scholarship. They were working in the very large classes which were being introduced as the new heavy work load was taken up. This created the second problem, that of the bright children who could not be properly challenged and extended in these overgrown and rapidly expanding schools. The able pupil often became bored and apathetic or even disruptive.

The slow, non-studious learner and the bright child mentioned above made the work of the teachers very difficult. It caused them to introduce the practice of streaming so that children of similar general ability could be taught in one class together. The intakes were divided into ability classes of around the same age.

The problems were similar in other European countries where education was also being rapidly expanded. It was just the problem of the new intake of retarded children in Paris, that caused the educational authorities to appoint Professor Alfred Binet for the work which led to his introduction of the intelligence test. He felt it essential to make special provision in separate classes for retarded children, those who had rarely been to any school in the previous age when schools had been largely for scholars.

There was an obvious answer. Accept more of the able studious children into the many good schools which continued in the older private sector tradition. In England in 1893 Sir Robert Blair, addressing the same problem, introduced the London County Council scholarship scheme (free places at public, grammar or secondary schools for able studious children so that they need not be limited to the learning pace imposed by this great extension of education to children of all ability levels that was going on). He said, 'Britain was the first nation to recognise the importance of making special provision for the education of her ablest children; it must be our aim to do this without distinctions of wealth, influence and social class.' This sums up very well the educational morality which prevailed when I came into the state educational system around 1920. 'Educate all but make sure the small but important proportion of high flyers get a chance to develop to their much higher potential.' The private schools (some called public schools) were independently financed by charities and by parents of scholars. They had evolved and specialised so as to get the best from clever and highly motivated children. The first of these public schools and grammar schools had originally been set up as charity schools for poor able scholars but they had gradually become fee-paying, specialist, academic schools where the scholarship students were a minority. Over the years many of them had become centres of excellence which were a good preparation for higher education.

'Let us make sure that these schools return to their original principles and give free or local council funded places at least to the brightest of the pupils from the "Council Schools" as the new non-paying schools were then called.' This was the thrust of the enlightened educationalist before the First World War and for some time afterwards.

What I seem to remember from those days is that all those not privately educated went to state schools, a large proportion, nearly all, became literate and numerate, got a smattering of British history, an idea of our present civilisation, British and some world geography, religion and a sense of discipline and good manners. They left school at 14 to go and work in service, in a shop, a factory, or on a farm. There was almost no truancy and there was order and rather harsh discipline with much caning, in all schools; the higher in the educational hierarchy one went, the harsher the discipline.

Studious, bright boys and girls from poor families got scholarships and thus free places at secondary schools, as they were then called. These schools taught at a faster pace, had an atmosphere suited to serious study, and better paid, more able and educated teachers. The pupils would later take a School Certificate or the higher Matriculation examination and if successful, later an Intermediate one. At this they could qualify for a paid place if the parents had the money, or earn one of the many free places at a university. During this phase teachers felt professional pride in getting as many pupils as possible as far up the educational ladder as they could. To get children into the local grammar school from an elementary school was seen in the same way as modern teachers see getting pupils into university, a matter for pride. Many misguided teachers today would take the reverse attitude and say that the children were being 'creamed off' to the disadvantage of the school they would have gone to if they had been less studious and teachable.

The advantage to a less successful student of limiting the progress of successful ones who could do better elsewhere is rarely explained, but it is asserted without explanation that having a brilliant student in a class, chugging along at an average pace, helps the less able in some way. In my own experience it merely discourages them. If the idea is that the bright children could 'help the others' scholastically it seems unfair as I have said earlier; the state compels parents to see that their children are educated so that they can learn what will be most useful to them. They are not conscripted as unpaid teachers.

The Universal Education Phase described above lasted to and through the Second World War and gradually merged into the next phase.

Phase 2: the 'select for ability not class' phase

The enormous apparent success of the socialist and communist movements around the world between 1917 and the 1960s had its effect on the next period. It is easy today to forget the way it was in those days before Kennedy stood firm over Cuba. Communist dictatorships had rapidly industrialised some countries and one had become a world power. They seemed united and between them they commanded much of the Earth's surface. And many of the old colonial countries were choosing socialism or communism as they became independent. Post-imperial Britain was losing its nerve, its empire and a lot of its trade.

In Britain the scholarship system had spread and developed. Many more bright, studious pupils from poor, motivated families found places in the schools that were suitable for them. But the richer parents could still obtain a place for a child who merely passed the (less severe) entrance examination. As the climate of opinion changed under the influence of Sir Cyril Burt, these lower entrance standards for the children of the rich were seen as unjust. So the next educational policy changes, those recommended by Sir Cyril, had the aim of eliminating the influence of parental wealth from the state system. There were to be secondary schools for all, not just for all the children of the rich and the bright ones of the poor. However, recognising the great range of difference in educability, the new secondary schools were to be of three types, secondary modern for the lower ranges of ability, technical for those likely to be suitable for work in industry, and grammar schools for those with further academic potential up to university grade. Gradually the selection process became more objective and fairer. In the state system at the secondary level, it was to be pupils' ability alone, and not parental affluence, which decided the placing of children in the various levels of secondary schools. The grammar schools, those which prepared for higher education, were nationalised as it were and funded by taxpayers rather than parents.

In order to make this selection really fair, to eliminate any suspicion of class bias, the previous system of selection by examination would not do. It was known that many bright and highly educable children who came from poor homes were underachievers. They did far less well in academic examinations than was to be expected from their real underlying potential as expressed in intelligence tests. So the scheme at the secondary from primary selection phase was to use only the fairest known means of selection, the intelligence test. The test was applied between 11 and 12 years old. The examination was called the eleven plus. Because of it many able children got to good schools who would never have gone otherwise. The proportion of working class entrants went up and that of middle class entrants went down. And many of these children from poorer families later went on to universities. (At the secondary to university selection boundary the examination remained the key. The Advanced or A level examinations replaced the Intermediate examination.)

All changes made by governments create winners and losers. It was an outcry from the influential losers that caused the next phase.

Phase 3: the anti-selection phase

Of course, a majority failed what was sometimes a single chance, the eleven plus intelligence test. Though the fairest method of selection then available, this test was not perfect and there were a number of well publicised cases where 'eleven plus failures' went on to perform well at university level (proving two things: that the one-shot early selection was doubtful, and that the eleven plus barrier was not impenetrable). These exceptional cases caused reasonable dissatisfaction and attracted disproportionate publicity which was not balanced against the great majority of cases where bright, motivated students, regardless of parental wealth, got into excellent schools where the standards and traditions were much more suitable for them than those they would have enjoyed without the selective system.

Much of the effective dissatisfaction with the 'eleven plus system' was caused when prosperous and highly vociferous middle class parents found they could not continue the family tradition and get their son or daughter into the local grammar school because they were not clever or studious enough. Most (by no means all) manual worker parents were not, at that time, much worried by such an eleven plus failure (nor very vocal if they were). Some I knew were worried by their child's *success* in this sphere. They did not want the 'lah di dah snob school' for their children.

However, middle and upper class parents who previously had stoutly endured the 'discrimination' of the fee-paying system were soon mobilised by egalitarian zealots to join an outcry about this 'unjust discrimination' when they could no longer buy a place for their child. The eleven-plus was soon an anathema. Instead of improving the test and tackling its one-shot imperfections by arranging to provide later chances for 'late developers', it became a political dogma that all selection below the university stage was unjust, divisive, and elitist. Somehow 'divisive' and 'elite' had become pejorative words. An elite, ('the choice and flower of society', *Oxford Shorter Dictionary.*) is not obviously a bad thing and dividing children into age classes is no less divisive than dividing them into ability classes. No evidence for these odd meaning-shifts was ever produced. No one told us what was wrong with chosen elites like doctors, engineers, lawyers or other professionals, or explained how a school can be run without dividing the children up in various ways.

Education politicised

Politicians and the media soon saw a chance to score what they fondly believed were publicity and popularity brownie points. The abolition of secondary selection became a political policy. It started in the '60s and was duly carried through as legislation. Disgracefully, it even became all-party policy for a time. The solution was to be a new kind of school called the comprehensive secondary school. Without so much as a pilot study to work out methods and solve the great difficulties, without any monitoring to find out what sort of education they provided, despite the fact that public opinion was against them, despite the enormous scale and expense of the changes required, despite prolonged obstinate local opposition in many places from parents and teachers, there began a long, painful period during which many overlarge, badly designed, poorly organised, undisciplined, new comprehensive schools were built, staffed and filled with an indiscriminate mix of pupils of all sorts. Many hundreds of excellent secondary and grammar schools which had built up their traditions and their specialist excellences over many generations were disbanded or bundled into the social mixing machine with other schools with lower standards. They were swamped with mediocrity by political zealots in local authorities.

Some of these comprehensives use streaming (separating into separate classes for generally fast and slower learners) or setting (doing the same but according to the subject of study). But the extremist form, invented by the zealots, the mixed-ability class in which all pupils were kept in a lock-step with their age mates, became the next dreadful fashion. This educational vandalism took quite a long time, 20 years. It continues today. There are, it is true, a few obstinate, hardy, survivors; centres of excellence, grammar schools and public schools which have held out and retained their traditions against all the odds until now. And, of course, the excellences (pejoratively labelled as 'inequalities') which had been thrown out of the door in many comprehensive schools crept back through the window in some schools in favourable districts. This always happens. The good comprehensive school today is very good, the worst is appalling.

The present climate is, happily, more favourable to educational selection because real doubts about this disastrous programme are beginning to be felt. It is very puzzling that the teaching profession via most of its unions and a lot of the media took it for granted that selection at primary and secondary levels of education is 'elitist, and divisive' meaning 'bad'. These new ideas were and are quite out of tune with majority public opinion.

(Through the years since, whenever there has been an opinion poll, there has always been a majority in favour of selective schools.)

The 'progressive education' phase

The progressive trend in British education overlapped the three other phases mentioned above and was even more damaging. The controlling elites in education were, as I have said, cut off from any effective input from its clients and paymasters, parents and the general public. They were also insulated from government influence by the layers of bureaucracy described earlier, so the teaching establishment was open to a series of fads and fashions in education which were introduced on the basis of quite novel and untested educational theories.

These ideas spread very rapidly and were introduced into educational practice, again without any properly controlled experimentation or subsequent monitoring. They spread simply by repetitive, unchecked assertion and soon began to be taught at the teacher training colleges as though they were the standard methods which had been established by generations of teaching practice.

One among these highly influential 'progressive' fashions was the 'discovery' method. The notion is that every child shall start from scratch and find his way to an understanding of, say, arithmetic or meaningful speech on his own and without the help of the learning sequences and structure which teachers down the ages have developed to simplify and order the learning process. The 'new' mathematics was a complete revolution in the way of expressing mathematical truths which cut every child off from the bulk of past mathematical literature. As Dr Rhodes Boyson points out, the aim was to let every child try to understand the deep theoretical basis of number theory, such as is used and needed only by professional mathematicians. What 95 per cent of children need is to be numerate enough to calculate wages, income tax, mortgages, housekeeping and the like. The insistence that they must first master the intricacies of number theory was impractical, and after a lot of wasted time and innumerate graduates the fad is at last in retreat.

Another damaging educational fad was 'the play way'. It was asserted that children should not need to make any effort to master the material but that all needed knowledge could be pleasantly and amusingly acquired by well designed games and play. There was to be no work or effort, no strenuous study such as had been practised by scholars back to classical times. It was all to come naturally. The name of the new game seemed to be to look at what teaching practices and methods had arisen over the generations before and do whatever was most different.

There flourished a plethora of meaningless catch-phrases like 'child centred education', and the notion took root that the teacher's only duty was to amuse and occupy the child and offer it 'learning opportunities' rather than actually to guide its learning, ie, actually teach. This was the new wisdom and all the previous teachers had been stumbling about in the dark. Humility was sadly missing among those teachers who were influenced by these doctrines. The penetration of the academic establishment by these curious ideas can be seen from a Ministry of Education Consultative Committee document from 1931:

'The curriculum is to be thought of in terms of activity and experience rather than of knowledge to be acquired or facts to be stored.'

The Plowden Report was probably the document which did most damage to the educational system. Children were to 'find out' they were not to be 'told' or 'taught'. One has to ask the question, 'If this is so who needs schools or teachers?'

There can be little doubt that the production of a literate and numerate population is one reason why, unlike all previous human lifestyles, our lifestyle enables us to afford to devote enormous sums and human resources to the vast and expensive education industry that we have built up.

This is our justification when we command the attendance and attention of every child for ten years of their life. Yet the attitude towards learning to read is exemplified by dicta such as 'no child should be induced to learn until it has evinced reading readiness'. The child was not to be persuaded or advised to learn to read. It was not to be 'pressurised' by having the advantages explained. The teacher has to wait patiently until the child's own curiosity drives it to feel the need.

Progressive education – the results

In his book *The Crisis In Education*, Dr Boyson noted some alarming facts. It appears that state education as recently practised has sharply reduced literacy rather than increased it. Nineteenth century reading tests that seem to him to be more severe than modern ones show that 79 per cent of Durham and Northumberland miners could read in 1840 and that 92 per cent of adults in Hull in 1841 were literate. He quotes R. K. Webb as of the opinion that three quarters of the working class in 1830 were literate. Webb's figures of school attendance fit the hypothesis that school leavers were almost all literate. He is of the opinion that universal literacy was achieved in Britain at some time between 1880 and 1939. The peak seems to have been reached in 1930 when all but a few clearly retarded children could read. That accords with my own memory when I was at school. I remember no one at my slum district school in Plumstead who could not read.

In 1966 a National Children's Bureau survey of 10,000 children of seven years revealed that 37 per cent needed primary level remedial teaching and a further 10 per cent had barely begun to read. Nearly half were not able to read at seven years of age. This did not prevent the publication in the following year of the Plowden Report which, in Appendix 7, proudly reported 'a remarkable improvement in the standards of reading in the 11 year pupils between the years 1948 and 1964'. No one in the educational establishment seems to have questioned these contradictions.

Dr Brian Start and Mr Kim Wells of the National Foundation For Educational Research published a report entitled *The Trend In Reading Standards* in 1972. A test of reading and comprehension was given in over 7,000 pupils (11 to 15) in 300 state schools. It showed that the standard of 11 year olds had been level until 1964 and then had fallen. The very bright 11 year olds were three months behind their equivalents in 1964, the middle group were six months behind and the least able group were three and a half months behind. Even these results have been criticised as being favourable to the later test. Truancy had gone up and it was probably not the most literate who skipped the test. Dr Boyson, who saw me when he was a junior Minister at the DES, says that it is now generally agreed that 6 or 7 per cent of British school leavers are illiterate and another 13 to 14 per cent are semi-literate.

Another very probable result of progressive educational fads combined has been the decline in order and discipline in schools. This has been especially harmful to the prospects of the clever studious child. I have sat in a number of modern secondary classes in mixed ability schools where there had been constant chatting and inattention with occasional need for the teacher to shout. The teachers were clearly competent but there was not the order and calm necessary for serious learning or study. At least a third of the students in these mixed ability classes were doodling or daydreaming, about half of these as I made out because they were lost and uncomprehending and about half because they were bored with material and questions they had long mastered. There is little dispute that truancy has increased, and general class discipline has sharply declined since these new methods were introduced. Dr Rhodes Boyson quotes modern truancy figures as high as 30 per cent at the age of 15. There are constant press reports of complaints from teachers about the violence they often face from pupils and even sometimes from parents. Boyson gives numerous reports and accounts in his book of national studies which confirm the seriousness of this problem. My own brother-in-law was a teacher at a Deptford school where he suffered so much violence from pupils that he was forced to give up the job. There seemed to be nothing the authorities could do about the problem. He told me that in that school the limit of the aim was to get about half the children functionally literate by the time they either leave school or play truant so much that they might as well have left. This is the sort of school where the odd bright child is lost and abandoned for ever. But the cheerful egalitarian theory is that it would be wickedly unjust to all the other disorderly children if a clever, studious child were 'creamed off' to a school where order, discipline and real teaching could be arranged.

All the educational fads of the progressive trend were advanced with oft-repeated catch-phrases which could be used to back the unsupported assertions of its proponents.

The traditional method in any human group since the beginning of human speech has been to spread information, teaching, know-how, news, instruction by means of one-to-many communication groups. It is more efficient to inform or instruct 40 learners at the same time than to tell them all separately. It also helps if diagrams can be drawn or material written large enough for all the pupils to see. The blackboard and its successors was a sensible idea. It does not need an Einstein to see the advantage of these simple methods. But this had been the usual practice and the simple visual aid used by previous generations of educationalists. But the eager reformers castigated this as 'chalk and talk' teaching and replaced it by lots of little groups around small disorderly tables. This inhibits the disciplined atmosphere required for serious study. Each child gets only brief intermittent communication with the teacher as he or she circulates. The system works adequately with studious and orderly children and very able teachers, but in many cases it works very badly indeed and the classes are undisciplined and ineffective.

Together with this wholesale abandonment of traditional methods and standards was a decision to do away with the established subject boundaries and teach an undifferentiated mish-mash of Social Studies which was supposed to, but did not, introduce a knowledge of geography, history, law and morals and a sense what the world was like and what you needed to know so as to live in it usefully and comfortably.

I am happy to say that though the ideas behind progressive education are still current and doing their damage, they are on the wane. In the late '60s the inevitable reaction began. Things got so bad that a number of enlightened educationalists started a series of pamphlets they called the Black Papers.

Starting when the tide of progressive education was at its worst they began to attack these so called reforms in a healthily vigorous way. Professor Brian Cox, Dr Rhodes Boyson, Baroness Cox, Dr John Marks, these are some of the honoured pioneers. Without significant resources but with enormous flair, courage and energy they started the movement that began to stop the 'progressive education' rot. The response of the Press and of the educational establishment was instant and intensely negative. The writers of Black Papers came under aggressive personal attack in the educational Press, but to the utter astonishment of the tiny team of reformers themselves, they found after a year or two that the more extreme styles were beginning to change and that there was the beginning a sensible return to more traditional methods. There is still a long way to go at the time of writing but we can now, in 1989, see clearly that the peak of the period of that aberration is past and sensible traditional methods are gradually being resumed in many schools and classes around the land.

The anti-elitist phase

The anti-elitist phase in education probably had its roots in the controversies, early in the century when IQ tests began to be used. It had always been known that there are dunces and scholars and the ways teachers told them apart were traditional and established. It was perfectly normal and effective in British secondary schools to split age groups at school up into what are now called 'streams' on the basis of their ability. There were six approximately age-based 'sub-forms' and each had A B and sometimes C versions: 1, 1B, 1C, 2A, 2B, 2C, etc. Pupils could be promoted to or demoted from these forms, usually at the year end. They could go from 3A to 4B or from 4C to 5B for instance. At the fourth form there was what was called the 'Remove', a special remedial form for those who had done especially badly in examinations. There were no visible harmful effects from these divisions; the social, friendship and sporting mixtures cut across the scholastic boundaries as though they were not there. There were first, second and third elevens for football and cricket and the boys from all scholastic streams mixed in these. At that time there was no idea that there was anything wrong or harmful about the streaming system. The Cs might have laughed at and despised the 'swots' in the A stream. The As might have pulled the legs of the Bs. It was the same sort of friendly joshing that happened between the football teams but much less vigorous because sport was a great interest and lessons were not. Anyone who suggested mixed ability classes as being 'less divisive' or more fair would not have even achieved the compliment of contradiction. A shrug and a 'screw loose' gesture would have been the maximum response from teachers, parents and pupils alike.

Quite how the modern meaning of the word 'elite' has become reversed, so that an elite is seen as something awful is not very clear. Some of the first serious writing about elites was from the Italian sociologist Pareto (1848 – 1923). He was tackling the problems faced by a country like Italy as it tried to establish democratic methods of government, after the Risorgimento. He pointed out that the older democracies had the *advantage* of established, experienced elites without which no modern government system could work. Italy, as he saw it, was in trouble because, at that time, it lacked that essential ingredient of the democratic lifestyle. They needed a cadre of experienced professional elites. My experience of educated and intelligent public opinion tells me that the world of academe and, to some extent, the popular Press are out of touch when they take it for granted that the public in general has ever become anti-elitist in sentiment or is against choosing and preferring excellence when it is perceived. There may be fair questions about the methods of selecting elites but no one but a trendy body of leftist, academic intellectuals who know little of the working world, can imagine that they are harmful or unnecessary. The new meaning of 'elite' is 'unfair selection'. By the new logic *any* selection was automatically unfair. There were to be no fast-tracks for high flyers. Let them grind through at the pace of the average, in some cases the slowest. We are lucky that calls for what logically follows, the abolition of those highly selective institutions, the universities, local councils or Parliament itself, were limited to the wild, outer fringes of the Left.

The peculiar and perverse set of ideas to which we give the name anti-elitism seem to apply only in the field of education. They may be traceable to a number of highly influential books which were written just after the last World War. According to Professor Ronald Fletcher, Professor Douglas Glass's book, *Social Mobility In Britain* and Olive Banks's *Parity and Prestige in British Secondary Education* were two of these. Jean Floud, J. W. B. Douglas and Basil Bernstein, also played an influential part in this great and questionable paradigm change. They began to argue the case that later developed into a whole educational philosophy in the mid-50s.

The sense of the argument was that to put pupils in different classes according to the general ability and learning progress was to form undesirable 'elites' of clever, studious pupils who were recognised and taught as such. The idea was that those who failed to get into these classes would permanently accept their academic limitations and stop trying to excel. They would thus be deprived of the equality of opportunity which they would have retained if they had remained in the same class with the high-achieving pupils, unaware of the fact that their performance was much better than their own.

Being lied about is good for you?

Another possible explanation for this preposterous doctrine is that the reformers were impressed by a single much publicised experiment, by Rosenthal and Jacobson in 1958, which claimed to establish the so called 'Pygmalion Effect'. After a test of children, teachers were given exaggerated expectations about certain children's ability. The children were falsely said to be 'spurters'. It was claimed that the children tended to meet the falsely raised expectations. Thus any knowledge about the promise of a child, such as test results, was said to be a 'self-fulfilling prophesy'. This led to the curious idea that the other children about whom no lies had been told were somehow worse off. Being lied about is good for you apparently. But instead of the obvious course, if this odd dogma was valid, ie lying about all the children to improve performance, the researchers recommended that any knowledge of the children's potential as revealed by tests should be kept secret.

The idea was that if teachers knew about the able children and thus, by implication, 'labelled' less promising children, they would do worse just because the teacher was informed about them. Further, since the faster progress of the 'spurters' was 'unfair', then it should be slowed down. The disadvantage to the other children was not shown by test or research, it was implied. So action had to be taken to stop all this spurting. The action was successful. Potential, real and false, was hidden and so undeveloped. Educational results fell off. But it was fair, so very fair.

As might be guessed the 'research' which was supposed to show this contradictory effect has been discredited and found to be unrepeatable. All the principal critical reviewers have pointed to decisive faults and errors in the experimental design (Thorndike, 1968, Snow 1969, et al.) The Marland Report says of the study, 'The study has been criticized on a number of counts, including the statistical methods employed and the testing materials and procedures employed'.

What is interesting is how widely and continuously influential was this one study which went against the grain of all previous work and suggested such strange counter-intuitive procedures. It is still widely quoted and treated as a law of nature. The many criticisms and refutations have been ignored. It was the one piece of research which supported the egalitarian, anti-excellence educational paradigm of those strange days of student unrest, hippies and flower power. It favoured the erroneous new 'anti-elitist' pattern in Britain, thus it survives.

It is sad that at this point I have to say something that is an absurdly obvious truism. Here it is. Every person who has ever dealt with a human baby or even the young of any mammal (such as a pet, perhaps) works to the simple rule of the teaching process. The teacher judges performance, recognises success and failure and gives appropriate signals to the person or animal being taught. They encourage success by smiles, pats, rewards and many other positive signals. They discriminate, they give negative 'try again' signals for failure, so that the baby or pet can learn what to avoid. Every young mammal has been subjected to this early learning process. It has had its performance judged and approved or discouraged by the older animals.

The central theme of the anti-elitist educational philosophy as it has now been developed is that the recognition and encouragement of successful study by a pupil is a harmful act because it discriminates against pupils who have not yet been so successful. When a teacher recognises ability and good work in one child it is 'labelling' all the other children as 'failures'. The theory goes on to say that the effect of signalling failure is not what every mother has always assumed (and observed), to induce further effort, a new approach, another try. The effect is said to be to discourage any further effort and the acceptance by the child of its permanent inadequacy. What a vast collective insult to the nation's children! What a lot of wimps 'anti-elitist' teachers think they are.

The suggestion is that effort and striving for improvement will be encouraged in a class where they are not noticed and approved. It is said to be essential to the learning process that teachers take a neutral attitude towards achievement and failure and all the pupils see themselves as equals at all times and in all respects.

139

Whatever the justice and morality of the new policy it does not work. The kids know or guess. They rank themselves for cleverness, and scholastic progress. Ask any schoolchild.

So many misguided teachers have been taught to forget their craft. They have been taught to arrange things so that there shall be no 'failures'. That seems to mean that there cannot be many successes. The way all creatures, including children, learn is by trial and error. They need to know error when it occurs, it has to be 'labelled'. No recognised failure, no learning. It is as simple as that.

It is very discouraging now, in 1989, that the Labour Party, having started to make itself an electable party by a number of very sensible policy changes, has failed to change the disastrous policy of rigid opposition to any educational selection other than at the university stage. I have heard socialist MPs frighteningly insisting on 'equality of outcome' in education and many are openly in favour of abolishing the independent sector in education, the only part that is really doing well. This amounts to removing the right of a citizen to spend his or her money in the most socially desirable way, on the education of his own children in his own country. (Obviously there is no way to prevent people in the EEC from sending children to be educated in a country with more concern for individual liberty.) It is hard to see any motive behind this curious policy except an envy-driven determination that if anyone wants to relieve the nation of an expense and buy some service that everyone else cannot or does not want to buy, it shall be made as difficult for them as possible. 'No one shall have it unless all can have it' is all right in the nursery, it is not sensible or possible with adults in a free society.

Rationing failure

Underneath nonsense we can sometimes find sense. In the 'no failures' or 'anti-labelling' policy there was a point, but it is absurdly and ridiculously over-stressed. It is true that there is a ration of failure which is too much and a very natural and sensible 'I give up' reaction to it. To go on striving forever for the unattainable is not in the interest of any person or animal and they all have to know when to give up. The big-boned 2 metre high lad can try till he drops, he will never do well as a jockey. The tone deaf will be wise to give up on the singing lessons. We all have to learn our limitations, to choose the profitable areas to which we apply our learning persistence. And we all have to find a way to know when we have reached our limits. It is no kindness to a slow child to encourage it in the belief that it can be a successful lawyer or an accountant if only it works hard enough for long enough. This is one reason why it is very unwise to expose slow learners to the full range of children's intelligence and capacity for study. It maximises the discouragement effect described above. This is the reverse of the effect intended by the reformers. What matters to a young, slow learner is how he compares with the kids he knows in his own class, not the ranking grown-ups put on the class itself.

Mixed ability teaching – a failed experiment

The educational dogma that mixed ability classes were in some way more just and equitable arose as an innovation and spread like a disease without even a pilot trial in the '60s. It was a part of the above mentioned educational 'reforms' under which comprehensive schools were established during the '60s and '70s.

I suggest that what the stupid cult of mixed-ability teaching has achieved is exactly the opposite of the honourable aim it set itself. The mixed ability class creates the very situation it is designed to avoid. If the teacher is fair to the average and bright children she will have to be taking them forward beyond the comprehension of the dull ones.

Mixed ability teaching confronts each teacher and child with the full range of variability in cleverness. This ensures the discouragement of the slow learners who cannot fail to know they are at the bottom of the class. And it makes sure that they are confronted with failure, all day and every day. They are certain to reach the 'It is hopeless, I give up' stage of the learning process. If the teacher holds the pace to suit the dullest she will be denying opportunities to the bright ones. If she tries to treat all the pupils as individuals she will have to divide her time into absurdly small segments and will be overstretched. Mixed ability teaching as a general principle was a bad idea. Probably any such novel general principle is wrong for education at the present state of our knowledge. Mr Donald Naismith, who did such very good work for education in Croydon and who is now Director of Education for Wandsworth, tells me that in his experience most teachers are utterly fed up with the mixed ability principle and that the main support for it comes from head teachers who are often under pressure from ideologically motivated politicians on local councils. The new status and greater influence of parent governors under the latest act should have a good influence here.

Is selection divisive?

I went to primary and elementary schools in a poor, working class district and was 'creamed off' to a grammar school in the days when this dreadful, unjust 'selection' was the normal way. Some small degree of friction, scuffles and quarrels I saw in plenty *within* all three schools but none, absolutely none, *between* them. I strongly suggest that there is not the remotest justification for the claim that academic selection 'divides' society in any non-trivial way.

The commonsense fact remains that all learning involves responding to signals of failure and success. If you hide under-performance from teachers and pupils, neither can correct them.

Assertions about harm done by 'selection', 'creaming off', 'labelling', 'self-fulfilling prophesies', that are given above are going against all human experience and values, if we were to act on them we should destroy every kind of excellence and reduce humanity to a miasma of undistinguished homogeneity.

Yet this sterile rubbish is still the received view at some teacher training colleges. It has been passed on uncritically to several generations of teachers. No one outside the education profession, apart from a few vociferous left-wing politicians and trendy academics, believes a word of such stuff.

Many teachers have little experience of the working world where such ideas would be laughed at. But widespread and evidently harmful changes were made on the basis of the illogical dogmas quoted above. In fairness I ought to say that the teachers who absorbed these harmful ideas saw them as fair and humane. They fitted the egalitarian ethos of the time. It seemed fairer (and wiser) then, when militant, class-warrior communism was an advancing threat, that teachers should aim for a uniform result rather than developing and furthering the beautiful and fruitful diversity of children's talents and enthusiasms.

Teaching was seen as a convergent process, bringing all children towards a norm, the British Standard Educated Child. We were all scared of the communist bogey of class war. We all wanted to be in a nice, comfortable, safe, uniform, inhuman and impossible, 'classless' society.

In the new more integrated world we have a planet-scale communications system which is spontaneously struggling into existence. World citizens now see education as a diverging process. Having mastered the primary skills, children ought to fork out educationally as they go on and out to the diverging world of advanced education or to the proliferating specialist occupational roles of increasing diversity of today's working world.

Poor results from mixed ability classes

Has comprehensive education and mixed ability teaching fulfilled the promise made for it? Four careful, large scale studies involving up to 380,000 pupils and 61 Local Education Authorities have shown that the combination of the few obstinately remaining selective, secondary modern and grammar schools has produced markedly better overall examination results than the comprehensive schools which have so nearly replaced them. The study by Baroness Cox and Dr John Marks shows this unequivocally. True, it was challenged by some anonymous, DES 'experts'. They were part of the educational cabal which, at the time, had presided over the dismantling of the traditional system which had evolved since the Middle Ages. However, the criticisms were designated as confidential and were not revealed. When they did come out they were easily and completely refuted. Exposed as erroneous, they have now been withdrawn with apologies by the Department. The challenge to the Cox-Marks paper got much publicity. The withdrawal got very little.

Further I note that in Northern Ireland where the abandonment of traditional methods in education was not carried through, the examination results are better than in England where it was.

The origin of school classes

The whole idea of a *class* of pupils, when introduced as schools got bigger in the 18th and 19th centuries, was to get children into approximately similar groups where they were able to cope with about the same level of work. In a reasonably homogeneous class a teacher can specialise in a particular level and type of teaching which must vary with the ability and motivation of the child. In such a sorted class, there are no utterly uncomprehending pupils, getting bored and discouraged and taking most of the teacher's time. Nor are there under-challenged very advanced pupils. If they work hard, bright pupils cause envy and set discouragingly high goals for the others. Alternatively they hide their talent, become lazy and or disruptive as they waste time going over ground they have mastered.

It was from humane but misguided notions of 'social justice' that the radical educationalists of the '60s rejected the wisdom and experience their profession had built up over centuries. That the results have not borne out their hopes is very plain. The trouble is that they do not learn from their manifest failure. They have not monitored their work and compared its results with the previous system. The independent monitoring that has been done condemns it completely. The new style of education is causing widespread dissatisfaction at all levels. Parents, press, teachers, their unions, the government and employers are all dissatisfied with the state schools.

In Germany and many other First World countries where pupils move up according to ability rather than age, measured educational results are years in front of those in the educational authorities which have changed to this new non-selective system.

How to educate for today's world

Despite all the money spent on educational research we do not really know the best way to educate children who come to school with a wide range of different abilities and motivations to be prepared for the much more varied life before them today. The career roles for which children have to prepare today are changing and diversifying enormously. It is very unlikely that there is any single uniform 'best' method. Many different models and methods need to be tried. The one we can reject decisively after too long

143

and obstinate a trial is the mixed ability class. Another that is almost certainly wrong is the overlarge and often undisciplined comprehensive secondary school. By its very size and non-specialist nature it makes the task of the teacher too difficult. Only the very exceptional teacher can be all things to all children. There are not enough of these around.

To pull up out of the present confusion and low standards, where traditional schools have been destroyed, we need to select from greater diversity. Education should be an open innovative field where experiment (with careful monitoring, testing and subsequent expansion or rejection) is encouraged. Schools should be smaller and more diverse until, by trial and error, a new pattern more suitable to the state of our civilisation emerges. This should be moderated by the pressure of public demand expressed through public choice, rather than political demand (whether by local or central government politicians). If this came about, improved methods, results and viable patterns would soon arise, be observed and copied. Bad ones would die out quietly and non-politically as happens in most other services.

Perhaps there should be more money and status for teachers who specialise in the difficult problems such as retarded or unmotivated and disruptive pupils. Those who can succeed at the demanding task of getting the best from brilliant ones will be rare enough to be able to get similar incentives.

There should be a wide variety of educational styles which should exist and compete, side by side, each developing their own traditions, specialities and excellences. This is what the primary, technical, grammar, private schools and universities did in the past with great success.

This applies equally to provision for the retarded. I doubt they do better in schools where they can hardly fail to hold back the general pace.

All excellence, all talent excites envy as well as admiration, but intellectual talent is the only kind where it is held that early recognition and specialist teaching and fostering is socially harmful. Those who have campaigned for these damaging Procrustean educational principles should search their consciences. They have a great responsibility to bear.

Independent quality control

In industry and in many other spheres the principle of independent inspection has been found to be essential. In education the inspectorate comes largely from, is controlled by and part of the educational establishment elite itself. For many years it took on the colour of the damaging current paradigm and stoutly defended it against a succession of Ministers and Secretaries of State. This is very hard to avoid where there is no market and the producers or suppliers of any service can capture the commanding heights of the bureaucracy which administers it. Things seem to be better today. The school inspectors are doing their job better than they were, but can such a service be effective when it originates from the producer side?

I suggest that the DES quality control system itself should be studied. The examination, career and subsequent social behaviour outcome as seen in pupils should be assessed by independent authorities from outside the educational profession. A one-off survey as to how well the system of educational quality control actually works would be good. Professional management consultants might do the job. HM Inspectorate, as it is today, seems to have improved greatly but and has shown especial concern in the area covered by this book, clever children. But it seems to me that the future recruitment of inspectors should be from a wider range of backgrounds. The management of this vital service needs to be more influenced by consumer interests, parents, employers and other groups who depend on the school leavers and graduates that the education system produces.

The new act is a bit coy about comparisons between schools. It is not made easy for parents to get the information upon which to base comparisons. Let all the results be published so that parents' choice of schools is based on clear, comparative, local statistical results. Leave the choice of service with the consumers who require, pay for and thrive or fail as a result of the service. These are the parents, pupils and eventually those who have to fit the school leavers into contributing roles in an ever more complex society, the future employers.

The results of schooling will be measured under the 1988 Act. The success of a school is the achievements of its output relative to its input. Schools with below average results in respect of the *progress* of students along the National Curriculum, not just the average level reached, is what should be revealed.

A poor record, after local variables have been allowed for, in the employment and career success of their pupils should also be exposed. These data should be widely and conveniently published and unsuccessful, undisciplined and ineffective schools should be allowed to diminish or be closed down as parents choose others. This is what happens to any unsuccessful organisation in the private sector. No one thinks it unfair if league tables and 'best buy' guidance is published by consumer magazines such as *Which* in the case of far less important purchasing decisions when private firms are concerned. What is the justification for allowing schools which provide a vital service, to hide or fudge their failures? If the act works properly, successful popular schools will grow and establish branches. Dud schools which turn out uneducated unemployables will fade quietly away. The educational service should be subject to the same discipline to which, in the end, all other services have to submit. The teaching profession has no warrant for its claim to be judged only from within its own ranks. Its results are not good enough.

This concludes the review of the various phases of the changes in educational philosophy over a number of generations in this century. The latest phase, which is beginning right now, is that of yet another centrally organised reform, the National Curriculum. The gross inadequacies of the system up to the present (1989) are now being so widely recognised that government has had to do something. The 1988 Educational Reform Act is the result.

Unfortunately schools and other educational institutions and systems evolve slowly. Excellence cannot be achieved by legislation or regulation. Talent and ingenuity often go into getting round them and avoiding change. What drives the evolution towards excellence is a pleasure-pain system, incentives, rewards and, yes, punishment – lazy or ineffective heads and teachers losing jobs. The key to success is going to be the incentive systems devised and the closeness of their connection with the measured improvements achieved. The damage that has been done since the '60s will not be so easy to repair.

British education in transition

THE 1988 EDUCATION REFORM Act (ERA) was passed as a response to widespread public dissatisfaction with British education in the maintained sector.

On the whole, the more educated the parents are themselves, the greater has been their dissatisfaction with the way things are. Apart from those who speak for the teaching profession itself, who have been almost aggressively complacent, there is not much approval of the service that is supplied.

The new act has the aim of making a great change. The source of authority is about to change. The influence of the parents can, if they are active and know their way around, become greater and that of the local politicians and educational unions correspondingly less. The parents' avenue of influence will be via the parent governors of the school board. The way to trigger changes and to have the needs of a bright child better provided for lies along this path. All those interested in educating children in Britain need to know something of this new Act. I shall relate my review of it especially to the really promising child and how the Act affects such a child.

The Act requires that every pupil at a maintained school shall be taught according to the National Curriculum which is outlined below. There is a provision for exceptions where pupils are certified to have 'special needs' and, as will be seen later, this can apply in the case of gifted children. In such cases the requirements of the act can be suspended or suitably varied.

There has been a lot of public dissatisfaction in many areas about the oddities of a minority of educational authorities. There is now something that can be done by parents in such cases.

The new hierarchy of responsibility in education

The links of the hierarchy of responsibility for the implementation of ERA will be as follows. This is the chain along which the parent will now have to work to get changes made or complaints rectified (or, of course, to do what is also very effective, to praise excellence in education where it is seen).

Comments, suggestions and complaints should be taken up with the teacher first. If no agreement is reached then the school head should be approached, then the chairman of school governors (some of these will be parents themselves). The next step if still unsatisfied is to the Director of LEA (Local Education Authority) and beyond that the local MP and or the Press. School boards can in future be much more influential than they have been in the days when they used to be packed with local politicians and trade union officials with ideological fish to fry. There is a condition, however. A succession of public spirited parents must come forward as the school-children pass through the system. There is a turnover factor. If a flow of new keen parents does not come forward things may drift on much as they were.

This is a simplification of the provisions of the 1988 Act on school management which must have interest for those concerned for promising pupils. A copy of the Act itself should be consulted for the closer details.

There will be two main classes of State schools, schools maintained by Local Education Authorities (LEAs) and grant-maintained schools, those maintained by direct grant from the DES.

Local Authorities responsible for schools must have approved schemes by which schools, which are now to be managed by the school governors, will be allocated an appropriate share, based on pupil numbers, of the Local Authority's general schools budget. The individual school's budgeting and financial management will be delegated to their governing bodies. Parents with a real interest in education are likely to favour this downward delegation of budgeting and managerial authority. These schools will be funded in proportion to the number of students they attract. Parents will be in a much stronger position than they were when it comes to choice of school. A school will be obliged to take pupils if they have free places. There will not be LEA 'rationing' by which less efficient and thus less popular schools used to be allocated pupils to make up the numbers and thus keep unpopular schools going. The governing body of a school is now to take considerable additional responsibilities. Its constitution is specified in the Act. There shall be the head and one (but not more than two) teachers, five parents and the previous or founding governors where the grant-maintained status is recent. After that parent governors will be elected by parents. Those with children at school in the public sector will have to make sure that those that become governors are motivated to raise and maintain standards.

We can expect that when each school's budget share has been allocated by the LEA and is managed by the governors of the school rather than by town hall officials, when schools have to attract pupils to raise their budget, that it will improve most schools considerably. It may lead to closures but that may be no bad thing.

The Act makes it possible for schools to opt out of the direct control of the local authority if a majority of the parents so decide in a ballot. Such a school, to be called a grant-maintained school, will be funded by capitation payments, its share per pupil from the Local Educational Authority and some direct grants from the Government. Its governing body would have to be approved by the Department and it is to be responsible for the school budget.

Schools which want to opt out of Local Government control must start the process either by receiving a petition from 20 per cent of the parents of registered pupils, or by a resolution at two successive meetings of the board itself. In either case the board arranges a secret postal ballot of parents which shall decide the issue unless the total vote is less than 50 per cent of parents eligible to vote. If less than 50 per cent of parents vote then a second ballot must be held which is to be decisive.

The Department has the power to appoint additional governors only where it appears that the governors are not adequately carrying out their responsibilities.

The National Curriculum (NC)

The Education Reform Act 1988 (ERA) aims to correct many of the manifest faults in British education. One of these was that there was no national plan as to what education was about, what in fact should be taught at which schools. The curriculum was a matter to be decided by the individual head and teacher. This worked reasonably well for a long time until the '60s but the egalitarianist trend and the trendy fads and fashions in British education mentioned on previous pages had much more attraction for teachers and their unions than for a public which neither understood nor agreed with them. Educationalists had lost touch with their market.

To restore public trust, a vital aspect of the new act is the National Curriculum, as it is officially called. This idea had all-party consent when it was first discussed in parliament. It goes against the past trend of education in Britain and turns to a model that has been successful on the Continent. It determines for the first time that compulsory state funded education shall have the subjects taught, the stages of learning and the testing standards set centrally by the national government.

ERA deals with the compulsory foundation curriculum which is to be mandatory for all pupils of state school age at maintained schools. It covers all British children from 5 to 16 years old except those that are classified as having 'special needs' as defined in the Act.

The curriculum must 'promote the spiritual, moral, cultural, mental, and physical development of the child and prepare them for the opportunities, responsibilities and experiences of adult life'.

These are set out as the implications of the policy in a DES pamphlet. Every curriculum in maintained (publicly funded) schools for those of compulsory school age must provide for these requirements.

- The principle that each pupil should have a broad and balanced curriculum which is also relevant to his or particular needs is now established in law.
- That principle must be reflected in the curriculum of every pupil. It is not enough for such a curriculum to be offered by the school: it must be fully taken up by each individual pupil.
- That curriculum must promote development in all the main areas of learning and experience which are widely accepted as important.
- The curriculum must also serve to develop the pupil as an individual, as a member of society and as a future adult member of the community with a range of personal and social opportunities and responsibilities.

A curriculum which meets these general criteria is an entitlement for all pupils. While specific aspects of the National Curriculum may not be appropriate for some pupils with special educational needs, and there is scope for special arrangements to be made for them, the general principles established in Section 1 of the Act apply to *all* pupils and must be reflected in all such special arrangements.

The National Curriculum includes three 'core' subjects, English, mathematics and science and seven further 'foundation' subjects, technology (including design), history, geography, music, art, physical education and at stages 3 and 4 (11 to 16 years) a modern foreign language. Some religion teaching, usually based on Christianity, is also mandatory.

The Curriculum scheme provides for attainment targets spreading over ten levels of attainment in each subject covering the full range (from 5 plus to 16) with clear objectives. It sets out programmes of study giving essential teaching in each subject and it sets assessment (testing) arrangements relating to the attainment levels.

The three core subjects cover the knowledge, concepts and skills required as the tools of learning, the essential foundation upon which all education is built.

Teaching does not have to be based on the above subject analysis as long as the full range of knowledge and skills is covered. For instance one lesson may instruct in history, geography and mathematics at the same time. This is called 'cross-curricular' teaching and it seems to be another innovation which needs careful watching.

The national curriculum is not seen as complete but merely as the essential minimum that a child should master. Such further subjects as career, health and social teaching are expected to be covered outside the range of the curriculum. (The NC is not supposed to take up all teaching time.)

Other subjects which have a suspicious ring of the 'schools are there to change society' ideology may be taught. They include such oddly named non-traditional subjects as 'economic awareness', 'political and international understanding' and 'environmental education' and curiously, what are called 'gender and multi-cultural issues'. We should not assume that these studies are taught in a biased way, but experience shows that the suspicion of political bias is not always unjustified. One has the feeling that sops are being thrown to some politicised zealots of the educational establishment who have extended the notion of what parents want their children to be taught at school and what schools should be doing in society.

ERA provides that the attainment targets in all the foundation subjects (which include the core subjects) will be set and amended from time to time by Orders coming from the DES. This means that we shall be following the continental practice in that control of the curriculum from now on will be national and from the centre. Can we be sure that there will not be a tendency for different political parties to modify the curriculum in line with their own ideas as they succeed each other in power?

The DES Orders mentioned will be arranged to fit a predetermined age structure called the key stages as set out in the following table.

The key stages of education under ERA

The table below is from the DES pamphlet. It gives an account of stages into which the education progress under the ERA have been broken down. It will be increasingly important to take these transition ages into account in planning movements from school to school or from class to class in future.

NEW CURRICULUM DESCRIPTION

Age	Description	Abbreviation
5 or under	Reception	R
5-7	Years 1 and 2	Y1-2
7-11	Years 3 to 6	Y3-6
11-14	Years 7 to 9	Y7-9
14-16	Years 10 and 11	Y10-11
16-18	Years 12 and 13	Y12-13

Broadly speaking, pupils in key stage 1 will be in years R, Y1, or Y2; those in key stage 2 in Y3-Y6; those in key stage 3 in Y7-Y9; and those in key stage 4 in Y10 or Y11.

Key stages are defined in terms of the **age of the majority of children in a teaching group;** and reported assessments must take place at or near the end of each key stage – ie at the ages of 7, 11, 14 and 16 for most pupils. For an individual pupil within a teaching group, the actual age at which he or she is assessed may be different.

Because a range of achievement is to be expected of pupils within a teaching group at any given age, the content of the Orders relating to each key stage will overlap considerably. For example, pupils at age 11, though typically achieving at around levels 3 to 5, might show attainment at anything from level 2 to level 6. Similarly, pupils at age 14, though typically achieving at around levels 4 to 7, might show attainment at anything from level 3 to level 8. Most attainment levels will therefore be relevant to more than one key stage, as will most programmes of study.

The assessment arrangements will likewise reflect the range of possible attainment at each key stage. They will require formal assessment and reporting at the end of a key stage, in terms of the levels of attainment a pupil has reached.

Range of variation in achievement

Unlike the present arrangments where mixed ability is the rule, allowance is to be made for the wide range of ability and achievement shown at each age level.

For instance, the level set as the target for a child of eleven, the point along the assessment tasks (the SATs) that it will be expected to reach is that which is reached by 'the majority of children within that age group'. The ages of children within such achievement groups will obviously stretch above and below the majority figure. Those who work with bright children know that many will be able to complete the course several years earlier than the last of the majority, the average child. The target will be the *average* apparently.

How will the promising child show up?

Here we get a problem for the very bright child under the NC. That method creates a very low ceiling which will tend to give excellence no chance to be expressed and recognised.

If we take the achievement level at a given stage as that which can be reached by 51 per cent of pupils, then we shall work down the advancement ranking to the average child. By definition 49 per cent will exceed that level. We go up the age groups to the tenth level at 16. The system will be setting the standard education ceiling at the level of the average 16 year old, the one of average intelligence and studiousness. This should be, theoretically a child with an IQ of 100 who is in the middle of the range in motivation and hard work. What he or she can do at 16 is the achievement ceiling of the NC. That seems an incredibly low level to set as the target for a new system. As we read the Act, there will be no standard on the NC which can reveal any progress beyond this point. The attainment targets are to be set to take account of the full range of achievement observed in the average child. Unless this anomaly is corrected about half the children will reach the tenth level and there will be no way of distinguishing among this top group as far as the NC goes. That will be a matter to be decided at the GCSE stage. Even apart from this anomaly, which will probably be corrected, the new examination, sadly, has come under fire because it is said to set too low a standard compared with the system it replaced.

Clearly, what is going to happen is that the top half of the ability range will be able to reach the tenth level earlier than 16, the really clever ones four or five years earlier. The problem is, what are the schools and teachers going to do about them? Leave them running on the spot for a year to two? Or find some method of acceleration.

These new arrangements came into force to be implemented gradually from the autumn of 1989. It is expected to take until 1991 for the full implementation of such a radical measure to be effected. I very much hope that the point above can be taken into account as the system is developed.

The assessment or routine testing at the four key stages (*average* ages 7, 11, 14 and 16) will not start until study programmes and attainment targets have been worked out, which may take some years.

Advance testing should be encouraged

The point to note for the parent of a gifted child is that they should be encouraged to take any of the key-stage tests as soon as they have a chance of achieving adequate marks. Parents should resist any tendency to hold back a bright or studious child by making it wait to take the test with its own class or age group. Good teachers will do all they can to help the able, motivated child to advance beyond its age group along these stages. Good heads will take pride in the numbers that exceed their targets and reach the 16 year target early. This policy will sharply underline the necessity for some form of acceleration, early entrance to sixth form work, for instance.

I have questioned the officials of Her Majesty's Inspectorate (HMI) on this matter and they tell me that the policy is equality of access. It is acceptable for pupils to be accelerated but, curiously, they may not be held back so as to cover ground they have not yet mastered.

The head teacher's job

Implementing the big, new ERA scheme is seen as the head teacher's job. There will be no central decisions about the allocation of time or even the subject divisions to be practised in any school. The programmes of study and the attainment targets will be based on what are called 'general assumptions' about the time allocated and the importance of various subjects but the details are to be arranged school by school. The head teacher is to see that the school meets the three requirements, those of national and local educational authorities and those of the school governors.

The National Curriculum is not to cover all of the curriculum. This leaves some room for schools to develop special classes in other areas of excellence but not perhaps as much as would be desirable. As I have said, modern industrial life requires an increasing diversity as the output of education, this calls for centres of excellence and specialisation. It would be good if, apart from the essential NC program itself, every school tries to find some specialist niche in which it would become a magnet school. Some of the specialities can be advanced versions of NC subjects, others might be many of the new arts and skills which are going to be needed.

The National Curriculum and the intelligent child

From the point of view of doing the best for and getting the most from the gifted child we must note this. To achieve excellence in many fields of endeavour, special, individual practice, training and education is needed from early childhood. This is true, for instance, of chess, mathematics, computer skills, foreign languages, acrobatics, dance, drama, athletics and many others. In such fields the ranks of those who excel contain a majority who started very early indeed.

The state-funded schooling system ought to take account of that and not leave the private sector to provide *all* the excellence. This applies especially in the learning of foreign languages. There is no field in which the advantages of early teaching is more vital. Children who grow up in families where several languages are spoken are often competently multi-lingual by the age of five. A defect of the ERA scheme is that plans for foreign language instruction to start at key stages 3 and 4. The first foreign language teaching begins at eleven years. It is very difficult to become really able in another language if the start is delayed that long. There should be room for pupils who show aptitude and are interested to learn other languages from the entry stage onwards.

It is at the stage of curriculum planning that any unusual group, like very promising children, is most likely to lose out. If some children learn a subject thoroughly and quickly they do not need to spend so much time on it. But curricular time tables cannot be worked out for every separate

154

child, at least not within any practical class size.

The DES recognise (para 4.8 *From Policy To Practice*) that most pupils in primary schools will need to spend almost all the time on acquiring knowledge, understanding and skills within the NC subject areas. However, they suggest that the need to cover other curricular ground should be fully explored. It is this that parents and teachers concerned about an especially promising child must emphasise. Ways should and must be found to allow the precocious child to escape the age lock-step which is so easily and frequently imposed because of time tabling difficulties of setting or even streaming or tracking.

Great difficulties are often said to arise from advancing children into older age groups, as in tracking (allowing pupils to work according to their curricular progress in mixed age groups). Stress is laid on the 'emotional immaturity' of forward, younger children. But, as I have said in earlier chapters, the harmfulness of the practice is implausible. It is a contradiction of some experience in the normal, extended family group, the happiest and most stable human grouping. Mixed age groups are more normal and natural than any other. It was the usual family pattern with mankind long before there was any education system. Many social workers in other contexts claim that the break-up of the all-ages extended family grouping has been socially harmful. Further, many observers have noticed that bright children themselves seek out and befriend older children, and often prefer the company of adults. Also there are numerous examples such as the Johns Hopkins University in the USA where a great range of ages mix in the same classes in advanced mathematics without the slightest evidence of harmful results over many generations. The solution, quite usual in Germany, the USA and many other highly successful school systems, tracking, must not be lightly rejected. Tracking is simply the long proven and widespread system of advancing pupils according to attainment levels rather than by ages.

Under ERA it is expected even at the secondary stages (years 7 to 9) that most of the time will be taken up by the National Curriculum together with religious and social education.

I have shown that this will be wrong for about half of the children, and it will be monstrously wrong for the bright, studious child. As I have said, many of them will be able to reach the attainment levels several years earlier than average children and will need to be advanced by tracking, streaming, enrichment, tutoring or some other means.

It is only at the secondary stage that it is anticipated that *all* pupils will need education beyond what is specified in the National Curriculum from key stage 4, years 10-11. If no provision for advancement is made before then it will be a tragic waste of precious early learning time for much of the nation's talent.

Those responsible for bright children should note paragraph 8.2 of the Act. It clearly states that different students will need to spend differing amounts of time on particular studies to reach a given level of attainment. Their curricula, it is stipulated, should reflect their speed of progress. That is good, and those who want to help the nation to find and use its best willing talents should see that school time tables reflect that stipulation. But the implication of what happens when the end of the short road is reached must be faced.

The targets and programs of study envisaged are to allow for and encourage progress while allowing for differentiation.

The ten levels of attainment in each subject are supposed to allow teachers, parents and children to understand what is expected of a child at each stage of its education. This sounds like an improvement and it will be if the intentions are reflected in the arrangements that are made by head teachers everywhere. It is to areas like these that school governors should be looking. Where there are doubts they should be wanting to know what is being done for the exceptionally able child. We have to remember what I said earlier. Heads in schools we have dealt with have reported that they have no such inconvenience as a gifted child at all. These pockets of Procrustean educationalists are still quite widespread. They will not change or go away overnight. The hypothesis of the self-fulfilling prophesy has been shown to be false when it says that teachers will harm average pupils by knowing about bright ones. But it is probably true when a head or teacher refuses to acknowledge, or provide for, exceptional teachability. To classify a very teachable child as average must surely stunt its educational growth. The head or teacher that consciously seeks mediocrity will surely find it.

Under ERA heads and teachers will still be free to pursue their professions in their own way, using their own methods and choice of materials. They will be constrained only in that their output results will be measured against general standards.

The NC is to be constantly revised and updated and this will be the task of the NCC (The National Curriculum Council). New social, technological and economic developments will be certain to dictate that necessity but in making provision for such changes and revisions there is always the risk of improper or politically motivated change or changes which result from the activity of single interest pressure groups. I have spoken of Dr Marks. He runs one such group, The Campaign For Real Education. It is in favour of an acceptable policy, a return to traditional Western Civilisation values in British education. He points out that what might be called 'entryism' has already begun in the administration of ERA. Some of the 'educational reformers' who have been identified with egalitarianist and leftist ideas in education are now on the committees which advise the DES on curricular and assessment methods.

It is hard to think of an answer to this problem except for continual political vigilance. It would be good if politicians of all parties could make a pact which outlawed the use of primary and secondary education, at least, for the purpose of changing ideologies or political systems. Those with ambitions to make 'irreversible changes in society' should work on adult educated opinion not on that of immature and plastic children.

ERA accepts that the task of the teacher goes beyond the education of the citizen, it includes providing a reliable measure of how well it has done that job. Past examinations such as the Matriculation and School Certificate, the GCE, the GCSE, have awkwardly and unwisely replaced each other, at intervals which are too short. They were set by independent organisations and were mainly aimed at selecting those suitable for later stages of the educational process. What is now to be introduced as yet another change is a system which extends right through the schooldays and provides an initial and three times updated profile of achievement at ten levels on ten subjects.

The last of these may be either the GCSE examination or it may the final level of the NC assessment. At the end of a school career, if the system works properly, every child will have been provided with four such ten-by-ten NC profiles which will rank it on the ten foundation subjects at various ages.

The levels of score obtained by each pupil on each subject will be determined by two means. At the key stages there will be objective tests, written and other examinations in the normal way. There will also be a system of teachers' assessment which will have a bearing on levels awarded. We shall have to be very wary of certificates which come from any non-objective measure of performance such as this. This would be true of any profession.

When thinking about teachers' assessments the parent of the promising child will need to bear in mind the evidence from the Marland Report that teachers are none too good at evaluating potential in children and that the brighter the child the less well they do it. If the results of intelligence tests conflict with these assessments there is need to enquire further. ERA assessment seems to be confined to educational performance it does not seem to envisage any tests of potential which may reveal under-achievement. The teacher's assessment would be more useful if it were informed by knowledge of possibly hidden potential. Many teachers have been surprised when they have been told the results of the tests we do in Mensa. A fair (but insufficient) proportion of them have readjusted their expectations from the child with good results.

Standard Assessment Tasks

Standard Assessment Tasks, called SATs, will be the key to assessment, they will be drawn up by the Schools Assessments and Examination Council (SEAC). If properly done they should set out a line of educational stepping stones to take the average child through its entire school career in every subject. There will be an item bank of these and teachers will choose the item or task that best fits the educational method employed. The SATs are to be tried out extensively in classrooms before they are finally adopted as the basis of assessment. This at least is good. The SATs for older groups will be more likely to be based on subjects. The SATs will be grouped as profile components and individual pupils' scores on separate SATs will not be given. Their overall score on the foundation subject will summarise these results.

The profiles with ten level scores on ten subjects will obviously be some help to teachers and parents in guiding the child's work during education. They can also be helpful when considered in the mass, statistically, as a means of quality control for the teachers and for schools. The comparative effectiveness of the individual district, school and teacher will be revealed by the statistics of the progress made at each stage. As long as this information is made generally available in a comprehensible, comparable form in each district it will be useful to parents when choosing suitable schools. A system used in the past, disgracefully, used to hide such results by making 'adjustments' in the school ratings to correct for what some politicians thought as social variables in the school intake. It is as well that future standards will be absolute and not deceptively 'adjusted' since the requirements of the new act, ERA, overcome this last point. Unadjusted results are required to be published to parents but individual results will be confidential otherwise. Schools will not be required to publish but will be free to publish the aggregate results at the seven year stage. After that age they will be required to publish them. However, local authorities will *not* be required to publish comparative tables of such aggregated results for the convenience of parents. Those authorities which do not, which fail to help parents to choose, will have to meet the suspicion that they are still bewitched by the out-dated 'banding' concept. 'Share the children out "fairly"; never mind the children or parents.' I am sure that such a policy will prove counterproductive. The gaff will be blown by some local newspaper and the parents will choose success even more firmly.

What will we learn from an NC profile?

The Act as it reads today seems, as I have shown above, to set *average* as the target and, if that is the case, does not augur well for the value of the qualification certificate that will be given to the child. If the targets are properly set and aimed at ranking all the children instead of the low-achieving half then the final ten levels should be drawn so as to divide the outgoing school population in to ten approximately equal classes on each subject. It will be a test of the system to see whether this is the case. The system will be less useful if it works out that, at the final level, there is too much clustering in the top few classes. If that happens the power of the system to select excellence will be limited. The value of the certificates will be correspondingly less.

This illustrates that the new system will be important for the kind of children about which this book is written. What will be best for them, their future employers and for the nation will be the system that most clearly, fairly and impartially distinguishes and signals excellence wherever and whenever it turns up. We must judge ERA by how well it does that.

It is unhappily significant that there is no emphasis in ERA as described in the DES pamphlet, on the usefulness of these achievement profiles to the most vitally interested recipient of the school output, the employers.

The assessment system is to be formative, to guide the teacher as to the correct directions in education; summative, providing evidence of progress; evaluative, providing statistical quality control of teaching. It is also designed to be informative in that it informs the parents, governors, educational authorities and 'the wider community' about the achievements of the school. It is also to help the teacher's professional development with the comparative information it provides. But nothing is said about the most important feature of all and the one which the pupil is most likely to value, the use of the assessment as evidence of literacy, numeracy and general competence which can be presented to a prospective employer.

I am afraid I have strong reservations about the value of these assessments to employers unless a lot more thought is given to this problem. I speak from a background of industrial management.

The value of any kind of certificate or assessment is set by the confidence it commands. The more easily it can be obtained the less value it has. The more complex it is the less useful to those who gain it and to those to whom it is presented. Any new system of such certification has to establish confidence and get to be widely understood before it is of any use to anyone. A long time must pass before any new system will be widely trusted. Its understanding has to spread out throughout the whole community of employers, right down to the millions of small businesses who engage a few people a year. It is a great advantage if it can be easily understood, if it enables comparisons to be made quickly and clearly. I have to say that in my judgment the new system of evaluation was not designed for and will not best serve its most important function, the vital one of simply and suitably fitting school leavers into the optimum niches in the employment market.

Many employers seem to be uneasy with or doubt the value of a previous change, that from the GCE to the GCSE. There are too many confusing grades which are not well understood. Too many who can show a GCSE certificate turn out to be unable to write a simple letter or do an elementary calculation. The examination coinage has been grossly debased and this has robbed every educated and able recipient of what he or she has worked for, trusted certification.

Even the modern honours degrees are often without honour where it most counts, in the job market. There are too many examiners who are ready to overlook elementary faults in English and mathematics in degree papers.

Margaret Orchard, the recruitment manager of British Petroleum was recently reported (*Sunday Times* 25 June '89) as saying: 'In some cases people who appear to have a very good education are not literate or numerate when put to the test. They are not coming through with the levels of competence that every child who left the old grammar schools reached.'

This sort of experience has led a group of large companies including Shell, British Aerospace and Abbey National to support a pilot graduate appraisal service, the preliminary reports indicate a very serious situation which cannot but cast doubt on the value of many university degrees. As an example, 60 per cent produced a wrong answer when asked to reduce '10,000.00 by 80%'. This example of the failure and consequent loss of faith in the examination system at the highest level is very worrying. One wonders what such a test at the level of GCSE and below would produce.

The new system started late in 1989 and will obviously take a fair time to 'run itself in'. The teacher shortages in some subjects is bound to cause delays. Since the first set of scores on the assessment tests are to be used to evaluate the SATs and, as it were, calibrate the system, they will not be published. It may be some years before the system is fully operational.

How will ERA improve things?

It may not be too late to derive from the complex new ERA assessment profiles a series of simplified and reliable broad qualifications which encapsulate what the employer wants to know about a candidate. A simple, reliable certificate that a prospective employee could write a page of prose for a letter or report without errors of grammar or spelling, or make simple calculations without elementary errors, might be more use to many school leavers than a complex series of profiles which require experience and study before they can be understood. One thing is sure, if teachers do not want to get into the business of certifying their output, that niche in the market will be filled somehow. Independent educational certification organisations are already setting up. They will fill the gap. Parents will be happy to pay commercial companies to examine their children privately if their certificates carry more credibility and improve employment prospects.

Unfortunately, as we see above, employers have come to distrust the vastly expensive national education system and its internal quality control. They are turning to these independent examinations simply because they have retained or returned to stricter, more relevant, simpler standards.

One can perhaps foresee that such independent quality control and certification may become the norm if the ERA system of assessment fails to gain the trust of employers. Parents and school governors may soon be pressing heads and teachers to adopt curricula that prepare for these examinations more than for the specified ERA tests and GCSE qualifications. It may be no bad thing if that were so. It would be one way in which the market for educated competent workers could impress its needs upon the education system.

Obviously parents of promising children particularly will welcome ERA and the installation of a standardised national system of staged assessments for the guidance of parents and teachers. They will want to give the new system time to be installed and establish its reputation with employers. But if, a few years on, the certification system has not established credibility, or is not well understood, they will be looking for alternatives.

No failures, no successes

To recapitulate: children's education is compulsory. It is a conscription system which demands 10-12,000 hours of every child's time at its most impressionable, fast-learning time of life. It is very expensive. We are heavily taxed to pay for it. It is not unreasonable for the public to set high standards for it and expect a lot from it. The sincere, sensible educationalist will see this and be very concerned that the educational certificates it issues are of value to those who have worked hard to get them. That unfortunately means that assessment will have to be strict and that not all pupils can qualify.

There will have to be failures. It is very hard to send a child away without the piece of paper its parents want for it. But if unqualified children are given certificates, the certificates cease to have value. All those that *have* qualified are cheated and the educational system in general has lost credibility. One reads many books and papers which indicate the belief that examination failures are a failure of the system. But failures are a reassurance. They indicate that examinations are doing what they are intended to do, certify study and mastery of learning. Without failures they are an expensive waste of time and effort.

It will be argued that every child should have *some* qualification. But we all know that the lowest of these, whatever it may be, that which any child whatever can pass, will be worse than nothing, a certificate of failure. We may express as much compassion as we like for the child who fails but we cannot help that child by injuring all those that have succeeded. Giving a hard-working, well-educated student a meaningless piece of paper after long hours of hard study and examination success is no answer. I see no way out of this dilemma. It is one of the problems whenever a service is delivered by the state. Somehow these questions are resolved easily at the delivery end in the private sector where strict quality control of any service is perfectly normal and people get used to being allocated roles and status according to their usefulness.

The simple lesson for the parents of promising children is this. Before you encourage your children to work hard to acquire a certificate or qualification of any kind, check up on the value that can be put on it when they get it. If it appears that it does not clearly discriminate between the able child who works and the less able one who does not, your children should not bother. If the examination will clearly show the top 2, 10 or even 20 per cent and other such grades below that, then that might, for your child, be worth the time and effort. If no failures can be seen the value will be in accord, zilch. A hoop makes a poor sieve. To work full time for ten years for a piece of paper that proves nothing seems to be a doubtful bargain.

How will ERA help the promising child?

Those who are concerned with the problems of the able studious child in the British education system will ask themselves how the new Act is likely to bring about an improvement in their education. Those in charge of education before the Act have not achieved much; will the introduction of a stronger parental influence really help?

It is going to depend very much on parents – not all parents but a few, self-selected activists among them, those that care enough to spend a lot of time and take trouble. Democracy works like that. Pressure groups have more effect than random people, very much more.

It is unpopular to say this but it is true that there are sub-cultures in Britain which put a low value on education. This has nothing to do with wealth or 'deprivation'. There are many families, some rich, some poor, which are unenthusiastic about, or even indifferent to, the education of their children. I do not condemn them. Their assessment of what education is doing for their children may be all too right. Their main idea is to get children through it and get them into useful employment as quickly as possible.

There is no pressure for educational reform from this quarter. The defence of egalitarian education fashion that has done so much harm, does not come from there. It is some, not all, politicians, some, not all, of those who speak for teachers and school workers' trade unions which defend the Procrustean egalitarian status quo. Too many senior academics who claim to speak for the higher educational professionals are ready to commit themselves publicly to 'anti-elitist' ideas which stifle talent and hurt the nation. They are guilty of clerical treason.

At the other extreme, parents from families, some rich, some poor, where there are aspirations towards and/or a continuing tradition of education are often very worried indeed about recent educational fashions. Many, not all of them, have high educational achievements. On the average over large samples, for both genetic and cultural reasons, such families are more likely to have bright, motivated, studious children than the general average. Many of these families have looked at the State educational system and they do not like what they see. They are engaged in what is called the 'bright flight' from it. They are ready to make painful sacrifices to get their children into private sector education when they can afford it, often when they cannot. When they cannot they become highly vocal and persistent agitators on behalf of their children with the schools and education authorities. We in the gifted children's movement know them well. They are insultingly called the 'pushy parents' by some teachers. There are many of them and they feel very strongly. The clamour from them is growing and it would be wise for governments local and national to take heed of it. And they are, many of them, being wise.

With the ERA changes in mind, if I were working in or dependent upon the state education industry, I would be re-assessing everything. If I sincerely believed in egalitarian education, 'progressive' educational methods, mixed ability classes and that my job was to achieve equal outcome rather than excellence and diversity, it might be wise to think of another career. The support for these ideas has come from some LEAs and their influence is diminishing. The hypothetical proletarian masses, if they ever really existed at all as a united body, have never been in favour of these policies, and they are not much bothered by the new climate. But the highly motivated parents who are keen on education and high standards will be very active, vocal and persistent indeed on the new-type governing boards. Schools with the poor records and reputations are likely to be avoided and fade away. The influential section of the British public is likely to become less passively tolerant of egalitarian, educational faddism in future. Those who still believe in it may stand and fight if they care to, but it is sure to be a lost cause.

Appendix 1

About Mensa

MENSA (Latin for table) is a round table society where no one has precedence. It is a world wide, non-profit-making society whose 90,000 members have only one qualification. They have all achieved a score on a professionally supervised, standard test of general intelligence such that they are in the top two per cent of the general population. Children may be members of Mensa if they can be validly tested for IQ.

Founded in 1946, in Oxford, England, Mensa seeks to bring together a small sample of the intelligent people of the world for social and intellectual communion, friendship and mutual stimulus. It conducts social, psychological and opinion research but has no collective policies other than to foster intelligence for the general benefit. It has international, national and local organisation and some members in about 100 countries. British Mensa Ltd is the British branch. It has about 30,000 members. Send applications for brochure and tests to MENSA FREEPOST WOLVERHAMPTON.

Mensa Foundation For Gifted Children

The Mensa Foundation For Gifted Children is a registered charity associated with and administered by British Mensa Ltd. It has been entrusted with the task of carrying out the Mensa aim of fostering intelligence for the benefit of humanity. It assists the parents of able children in the diagnosis of high intelligence by arranging intelligence and educational tests (free to those that cannot afford them) and by consultation, advice and action to obtain education for very promising children such that their potentiality shall be fulfilled for the advantages of the nation and the children themselves. Send applications for brochure and test to MENSA FREEPOST WOLVERHAMPTON. (Envelope marked 'CHILD'.)

Appendix 2

Some useful addresses

British Mensa Ltd and The Mensa Foundation for Gifted Children (For test and advice respectively) Mensa House, St John's Square, Wolverhampton WV2 4AH (Tel 0902 772771).

International Mensa 15, The Ivories, 6–8 Northampton Street, London N11 2HY (Tel 01-226 6891).

Able Children (enrichment packs for children) 121 London Road, Knebworth, Herts SG3 6EX (Tel 0438 815232).

Individual Organisational Development Agency (IODA) (Trained educational psychologists) Stanton House, 6 Eastham Village Road, Wirrall L62 8AD.

Department of Education and Science Despatch Centre (For publications) Honeypot Lane, Stanmore, Middlesex HA7 1AZ.

The European Council for High Ability Dr Pieter Span, Dept of Education, Univ of Utrecht, Heidelberglaan 2 3584 CS, Utrecht, Netherlands.

Eurotalent General Secretary, 33 Franklin Roosevelt Ave, 30000 Nimes, France (Tel Dialling code plus 66–64 82 51).

Independent Schools Information Service (ISIS) 56 Buckingham Gate, London SW1E 6AG (Tel 01-630 8793)

Gabbitas Thring Educational Trust Ltd 6 Sackville Street, London W1X 1DD (Tel 01-734 0161 & 01-439 2071).

Joint Educational Trust 15 St Mary's Walk, London SE11 4UA (Tel 01-793 0522).

National Association for Gifted Children 1 South Audley Street, London W1Y 5DQ (01-499 1188).

NAGC (Scotland) Mr Jeremy Snowden, 17 Ravelstone House Road, Edinburgh.

British Dyslexia Association 98 London Road, Reading RG1 5AU (Tel 0734 668271/2).

Appendix 3

Educational acronyms

We all have to get used to a new set of institutions and their new acronyms if we are to understand the changes we are to expect. And we have to if we are to make the Education Reform Act do the best for the most educable children. Here are the most important.

DES The Department of Education and Science
ERA Education Reform Act 1988.
NC National Curriculum
NCC National Curriculum Council. The body which sets the NC.
SEAC School Examination and Assessment Council.
SAT Standard Assessment Tasks. Externally imposed examination tasks set to match the NC.
TGAT Task Group on Assessment and Testing.
TVEI Technical and Vocational Education Initiative.

Bibliography

ABRAHAM W. *Common Sense About Gifted Children.* Harper. New York, 1958.

BARBE W. *The Exceptional Child.* Center for Applied Research in Education Inc, Washington DC, 1963.

BECK J. *How to Raise a Brighter Child.* Fontana 1970.

BLOCK N. & DWORKIN G. *The IQ Controversy.* Quartet. 1977.

BRANCH M. & CASH A. *Recognizing and Developing Educational Ability.* Souvenir Press. London, 1966.

BRANCH M. & CASH A. *Gifted Children.* Souvenir Press. London, 1966.

BRANDWEIN P. F. *The Gifted Student as a Future Scientist.* Harcourt Brace. New York, 1955.

BRIDGES S. A. *Gifted Children and the Brentwood Experiment.* Pitman. London, 1969.

BRIDGES S. A. *Gifted Children and the Millfield Experiment.* Pitman. London, 1975.

BULLOCK A. *A Language for Life.* HMSO, 1975.

BURT C. *The Gifted Child.* Hodder & Stoughton. London, 1975.

CLENDENNING Corinne P. & DAVIES Ruth Ann. *Creating Programs for the Gifted, A Guide for Teachers, Librarians & Students.* R. R. Bowker Company. New York and London, 1980.

CRUICKSHANK W. M. (Editor). *Education of Exceptional Children and Youth.* Prentice-Hall, Englewood Cliffs, N. J., 1958.

CUTTS N. E. & MOSELEY N. *Bright Children, a Guide for Parents.* Putnam. New York, 1953.

CUTTS N. E. & MOSELEY N. *Teaching the Bright and Gifted.* Prentice Hall. 1957.

DE HAAN R. F. & HAVIGHURST R. J. *Educating Gifted Children.* Univ of Chicago Press, 1957.

DEAKIN M. *The Children on the Hill: The Story of an Extraordinary Family.* Andre Deutsch. London, 1972.

DUNN L. M. *Exceptional Children in School.* Holt, Rinehart & Winston Ltd. New York, 1965.

DURR W. K. *The Gifted Student.* OUP. New York, 1964.

DURROW G. *The Gifted Student.* Oxford Univ Press. New York, 1964.

EYESENCK/KAMIN. *Intelligence and the Battle of the Mind.* Pan. 1981.

FANCHER R. E. *The Intelligence Men–the Makers of the IQ Controversy.* W. W. Norton & Co. 1985.

FREEHILL M. F. *Gifted Children Their Psychology and Education.* Macmillan. New York, 1961.

FREEMAN JOAN. *Gifted Children Their Identification and Development in a Social Context.* MTP Press Ltd. 1979.

FRENCH J. L. *Educating the Gifted, a Book of Readings.* Holt, Rinehart, Winston, New York. 1959.

GALLAGHER J. J. *Teaching Gifted Students.* Allyn & Bacon Inc. 1968.

GALLAGHER J. J. *Teaching the Gifted Child.* Allyn & Bacon Inc. 1975.

GOLD M. J. *Education of the Intellectually Gifted.* Charles E Merrill Books. Columbus, Ohio, 1965.

GOODENOUGH E. *Exceptional Children.* Appleton Century Crofts. 1956.

GOULD S. J. *The Mismeasure of Man.* Norton. 1981.

GOWAN J. C. & TORRANCE E. P. *Educating the Ablest.* Peacock Itasca. Illinois, 1971.

GRANT N. *Soviet Education.* Penguin Books, 1968.

GRUBB D. H. W. ED *The Gifted Child at School.* Oxford Society for Applied Studies in Education, 1982.

HALL T. *Gifted Children The Cleveland Story.* World Publishing Co. 1956.

HAVINGHURST R. J. et al. *A Survey of the Education of Gifted Children.* Chicago University Press 1955.

HEARNSHAW L. *Cyril Burt: Psychologist.* Cornell Univ Press. 1979.

HERSEY J. *Intelligence, Choice & Consent.* Woodrow Wilson Foundation. 1959.

HEWETT M. H. *Education of Exceptional Learners.* Allyn & Bacon. 1977

HILDRETH G. H. *Introduction to the Gifted.* McGraw-Hill. New York, 1966.

HITCHFIELD E. M. *In Search of Promise.* Longman, 1973.

HMI Series. *Ten Good Schools.* HMSO. London, 1978.

HMI. *Gifted Children in Middle and Comprehensive Schools.* HMSO. London, 1977.

HMI. *Mixed Ability in Comprehensive Schools.* HMSO. London, 1978.

HOLLINGWORTH L. S. *Children Above 180 IQ.* World Book Company, Yonkers on Hudson, New York, 1942.

HOLLINGWORTH L. S. *Gifted Children: Their Nature and Nurture.* Macmillan. New York, 1926.

HOYLE E. & CHRISTIE T. *Gifted Children and Their Education.* HMSO. London, 1974.

HUNT J. McV. *Intelligence and Experience.* Ronald. New York, 1961.

KERRY T. *Finding and Helping the Able Child.* Croom Helm. 1983.

McCLEOD J & CROPELEY A. *Fostering Academic Excellence.* Pergamon Press, 1989.

MARLAND S. P. *Education of the Gifted and Talented.* Report to the US Congress, 1972.

MARTINSON R. A. *Curriculum Enrichment for the Gifted in the Primary Grades.* Prentice-Hall. New Jersey, 1968.

NATIONAL SOCIETY FOR THE STUDY OF EDUCATION. *Education for the Gifted.* Public School Publishing Co, 1958.

NEWLAND T. E. *The Gifted in Socio-educational Perspective.* Prentice-Hall, 1976.

ODEN M. H. *The Fulfilment of Promise: 40 year Follow-up of the Terman Gifted Group.* Genetic Psychology Monographs. 1968.

OGILVIE E. *Gifted Children in Primary Schools.* Macmillan Educ. 1973.

OSTWALT E. R. *The Role of Parent in the Training and Education of Mentally Superior Children.* Kent State University Bulletins, Ohio, 1957.

PAINTER F. *Living With a Gifted Child.* Souvenir Press. 1984.

PARKYN G. W. *Children of High Intelligence: A New Zealand Study.* OUP. London 1948.

PIAGET J. *The Psychology of Intelligence.* Routledge & Kegan Paul. 1951.

PIAGET J. *Language and Thought of the Child.* Meridian. 1955.

PICKARD P. M. *If You Think Your Child is Gifted.* George Allen & Unwin. 1976.

PLOWDEN REPORT. *Children and Their Primary Schools.* HMSO. 1967.

POLETTE Nancy & HAMLYN Marjorie. *Exploring Books With Gifted Children.* Libraries Unlimited Inc. Littleton, Colorado, 1980.

POVEY R. *Educating the Gifted Child.* Harper and Row. 1980.

PRINGLE, M. L. KELLMER. *Able Misfits.* Longman. London, 1970.

REYNOLDS M. C. *Early School Admission for Mentally Advanced Children.* Council for Exceptional Children. Washington DC, 1962.

RICE J. P. *The Gifted: Developing Total Talent.* Charles C. Thomas. Springfield, Illinois. 1970.

ROSENTHAL R. & JACOBSON L. *Pygmalion in the Classroom.* Holt Rinehart & Winston. 1968.

ROWLANDS P. *Gifted Children and Their Problems.* Dent. London, 1974.

SEREBRIAKOFF V. *Check Your Child's IQ.* Mensa Publications, 1989.

SEREBRIAKOFF V. *Mensa, the Society for the Highly Intelligent.* Constable. London, 1985.

SEREBRIAKOFF V. *A guide to Intelligence and Personality Testing.* Parthenon, 1988.

SEREBRAIKOFF V. *The Future of Intelligence* Parthenon, 1987.

SHIELDS J. *Monozygotic Twins Brought Up Apart and Together.* OUP. 1962.

SHIELDS J. B. *The Gifted Child.* National Foundation for Educational Research. Slough, Bucks. 1968.

SPEARMAN C. *The Abilities of Man.* Macmillan. 1927.

STANDING E. M. *Maria Montessori: Her Life and Work.* Mentor-Omega Books. 1962.

STEVENS, AURIOL. *Clever Children in Comprehensive Schools.* Harper and Row. London, 1980.

SUMPTION M. R. *Three Hundred Gifted Children.* World Book Co. New York, 1941.

SUMPTION M. R. & LUECKING E. M.. *Education of the Gifted.* Roland Press. New York, 1960.

TEMPEST N. R. *Teaching Clever Children 7–11.* Routledge and Kegan Paul. London and Boston, 1974.

TERMAN L. M. *Mental and Physical Traits of 1000 Gifted Children.* Stanford Univ Press. 1925.

TERMAN L. M. *The Gifted Child Grows Up: Genetic Studies of Genius.* Stanford Univ Press. 1974.

TERMAN L. M. *The Measurement of Intelligence.* Houghton Mifflin. 1916.

TERMAN L. M. *The Gifted Group at Mid Life: Genetic Studies of Genius.* Stanford Univ Press. 1959.

TOFFLER A. *The Third Wave.* Penguin. 1981.

TORRANCE E. P. *Gifted Children in the Classroom.* Macmillan. New York, 1965.

TYLER E. L. *Tests and Measurements.* Prentice-Hall New Jersey, 1963.

VERNON P. E. *Intelligence and Cultural Environment.* Methuen. 1969.

VERNON P. E. *Intelligence and Attainment Tests.* Univ of London Press. 1960.

VERNON P. E. *The Psychology and Education of Gifted Children.* Methuen. 1977.

WADDINGTON M. *Problems of Educating Gifted Young Children With Special Reference to Great Britain.* Evans. 1961.

WALLACH M. A. & WING C. W. *The Talented Student.* Holt, Rinehart & Winston. New York, 1969.

WARD V. S. *Educating the Gifted: An Axiomatic Approach.* Ohio Merrill Books. 1961.

WECHSLER D. *The Measurement of Adult Intelligence.* Williams & Wilkins. 1944.

WILLARD A. *Common Sense About Gifted Children.* Harper. New York, 1958.

WITTY P. *The Gifted Child.* American Assn for Gifted Children. Heath Boston, 1951.

WOOLCOCK C. *The Hunter College High School Program for Gifted Students.* New York Vantage Press. 1962.

WORCESTER D. A. *The Education of Children of Above Average Intelligence.* Univ of Nebraska Press. 1956.

YEARBOOK OF EDUCATION. *The Gifted Child.* Evans. London, 1962.

Acknowledgements

IT WILL BE IMPOSSIBLE to acknowledge all those who have helped me, knowing or unknowingly, in the writing of this book.

Innumerable discussions since 1950 with thousands of those in many lands who were all clever children once, the members of Mensa in many lands, these have been my main source of inspiration and information. But here, in no especial order, I give the names of those who have been helpful while I was writing. These are the names which come most warmly to my fallible memory. Will those I have failed to mention forgive a grateful but forgetful friend?

My wife, Win, has helped and my colleagues in the Mensa Foundation For Gifted Children, John Walker, Clare Lorenz, Sheila Mole, Lyn Alcock, have been of great help with information, comments and contributions. Dr Margaret Pollak who is a paediatrician has been of very great help. The education psychologists, Dr Rosalind Myatt and James Stevenson have advised. Ken Russell helped greatly with checking and with the test. My friends, Sir Clive Sinclair, John McNulty, Jack Cohen and the Professors Ronald Fletcher and Stanislav Andreski have helped with advice. My son Mark, his wife Liz and especially my granddaughter Alexandra Julia, have provided me with practical experience of a very bright baby from birth. Margaret Borwick was most helpful in the early days. Harold Gale helped with his teaching experience.

I also want to acknowledge the helpfulness and interest in the problem of the officials of the Department of Education and Science especially HM Inspectorate. The Greater London Council have arranged school visits for me and I have had great help from Donald Naismith, the Director of Education for the Wandsworth Council. Sir Rhodes Boyson has helped me. Baroness Stocks and John Marks of The Campaign For Real Education have helped too with the informative conferences they run.

None of these to whom I am indebted are responsible for my opinions, mistakes or errors.

Index

NC = National Curriculum